HUMAN RIGHTS ARE WOMEN'S RIGHT

AI Index: ACT/77/01/95

ISBN# 0-939994-98-4

First published in March 1995
Amnesty International USA
322 Eighth Avenue
New York, NY 10001

Original language: English

Printed by John D. Lucas Printing Co.

CONTENTS

CORRECTION:

Page 67, 3rd paragraph:

We have just learned that Shaheen Sameie from Iran has been released from prison.

GLOSSARY

CEDAW	Committee on the Elimination of Discrimination against Women
CNVR	National Commission for Truth and Reconciliation [Chile]
COFADEH	Committee of Relatives of the Disappeared [Honduras]
CONAVIGUA	National Coordinating Committee of Widows of Guatemala
CREDHOS	Regional Human Rights Committee [Colombia]
DINA	Directorate of National Intelligence [Chile]
DINCOTE	National Directorate against Terrorism [Peru]
ELN	National Liberation Army [Colombia]
EPLF	Eritrean People's Liberation Front
EU	European Union
FARC	Revolutionary Armed Forces of Colombia
FENASTRAS	National Trade Union Federation of Salvadorian Workers
FENSUAGRO	National Federation of United Agricultural Unions [Colombia]
FGM	Female Genital Mutilation
FIDA	International Federation of Women Lawyers [Kenya]
FIS	Islamic Salvation Front [Algeria]
FMLN	Farabundo Martí National Liberation Front [El Salvador]
FORD	Forum for the Restoration of Democracy [Kenya]
FRUD	Front for the Restoration of Unity and Democracy [Djibouti]
HRA	Human Rights Association [Turkey]
HRW	Human Rights Watch
ICCPR	International Covenant on Civil and Political Rights
KLA	Khalistan Liberation Army [India]
KODIM	District Military Command [Indonesia]
KORAMIL	Sub-District Military Command [Indonesia]
LBH	Legal Aid Institute [Indonesia]
LDK	Democratic League of Kosovo [Yugoslavia]
LTTE	Liberation Tigers of Tamil Eelam [Sri Lanka]
MAR	Harmony Movement [Cuba]
MRTA	Túpac Amaru Revolutionary Movement [Peru]
MSM	Salvadorian Women's Movement
NLD	National League for Democracy [Myanmar]
OJAL	Organization of Young Free Algerians

OLM	Oromo Liberation Front [Ethiopia]
ONLF	Ogaden National Liberation Front [Ethiopia]
OWDA	Ogadenian Women's Democratic Alliance [Ethiopia]
PCA	Party for Communist Action [Syria]
PKI	Indonesian Communist Party
PKK	Kurdish Workers' Party [Turkey]
PNP	Philippine National Police
POW	Progressive Organisation of Women [India]
RENAMO	Mozambique National Resistance
SPLA	Sudan People's Liberation Army
UDHR	Universal Declaration of Human Rights
UN	United Nations
UNDP	United Nations Development Programme
UNHCR	Office of the United Nations High Commissioner for Refugees
UNICEF	United Nations Children's Fund
UNITA	National Union for the Total Independence of Angola
USA	United States of America

INTRODUCTION

Left: *Refugees from the war in Bosnia-Herzegovina arriving in Croatia. Hundreds of thousands of people have fled from appalling human rights violations in the territories of the former Yugoslavia. Women at risk of human rights violations have little opportunity to exercise their rights to peace, development and equality, the theme of the Fourth UN Conference on Women.*
© Howard J. Davies

Eren Keskin is a lawyer and a human rights activist in Turkey. Because she has defended alleged members of the Kurdish Workers' Party (PKK), the Kurdish armed group in conflict with the government, she has been repeatedly harassed. The harassment includes death threats — "We are measuring your coffin" went one telephone message — being shot at, physical assault by a police officer and arbitrary detention and ill-treatment to prevent her doing her job. Eren Keskin also faces a sentence of two years' imprisonment for "separatist propaganda" because she sent a message to the Belgian parliament about the conflict in southeastern Turkey.

Agathe Uwilingiyimana was one of the first reported victims of the mass slaughter in Rwanda in April 1994. She was the country's Prime Minister. She was killed by members of the Presidential Guard while sheltering in the United Nations Development Programme (UNDP) compound in Kigali, Rwanda's capital city. Her killing and that of other government ministers appears to have been planned well in advance by the military.

Angélica Mendoza de Ascarza, aged 70, has recently emerged from two years in hiding in Peru. She is the president of the National Association of Relatives of the Kidnapped, Detained and Disappeared, of whom there are several thousand in Peru. In September 1992 Angélica Mendoza's name appeared on a list of alleged supporters of the armed opposition, which was presented to the press by Peru's President Alberto Fujimori. A warrant was issued for her arrest; she went into hiding and began the fight to clear her name. In mid-1993 Peru's higher court ruled that there was no evidence to back the accusation against her. This ruling was upheld in September 1994; in

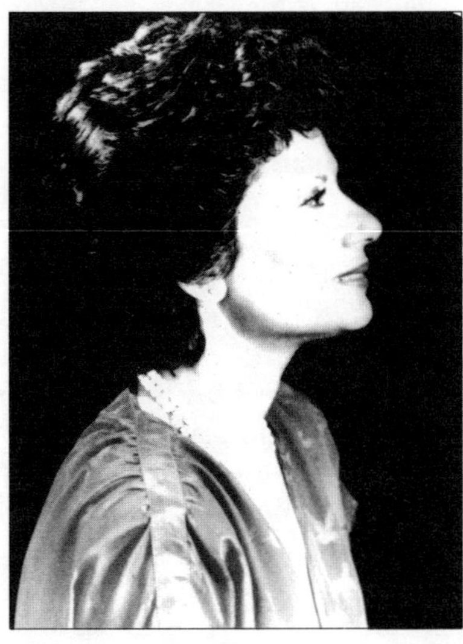

Dr Homa Darabi, Iran

the meantime Angélica Mendoza lived in fear of her life.

Aung San Suu Kyi has been under house arrest in Myanmar for almost six years because she dared to oppose the government. The party she co-founded in 1988, the National League for Democracy, won a landslide victory in the May 1990 elections when she was already in detention. The military government refused to recognize the results and arrested most of the party's leaders. She has never been tried. Her name and detention became internationally known in 1991 when she was awarded the Nobel Peace Prize.

In February 1994 Dr Homa Darabi went to one of the busiest streets in Tehran, Iran's capital city, tore off her headscarf and *chador*, poured petrol over her body and then set herself on fire. As the flames engulfed her she shouted: "Down with tyranny, long live freedom, long live Iran." Professor of Child Psychiatry at Tehran's National University, she had been persistently harassed by the security forces for failing to follow the strict Islamic dress code, culminating in her dismissal in December 1991. A talented and widely respected professional was thus forced into a life of inactivity. She chose to die instead and to make her death a protest for justice and freedom.

A mother lies dead, her hands stretched towards her child, in the Goma refugee camp, on the border between Zaire and Rwanda. As many as one million people were massacred in Rwanda following the death of President Habyarimana in April 1994. By August more than a million people had fled the country. © Jenny Matthews

These five women, from the five regions of the world, are or were exemplary women of the 1990s. They symbolize the millions of women for whom this decade has meant terror, deprivation and the imperative of fighting for justice, but whose stories have been largely hidden from history. Today, what unites women internationally — transcending class, race, culture, religion, nationality and ethnic origin — is their vulnerability to the denial and violation of their fundamental human rights, and their dedicated efforts to claim those rights.

Women are the invisible victims of the 1990s, the faceless masses filling the backgrounds on the canvases of terror and hardship. Most of the casualties of war are women and children; most of the world's refugees and displaced people are women and children; most of the world's poor are women and children. Most of these women are struggling to care for and protect most of these children. Human rights violations against women are rampant partly because they remain largely hidden.

The great failure of the world's community of governments is not just that they have been unable to guarantee women their social, economic and cultural rights — women's right to peace, development and equality is the theme of the forthcoming UN World Conference on Women — it is that they have been unable to prevent and in some cases have sanctioned the violation of women's civil and political rights: the rights not to be tortured, killed, made to "disappear", arbitrarily detained or imprisoned. Certain violations, such as rape by government agents, are primarily directed at women.

"While there has been steady progress in the articulation and implementation of women's rights in many countries, a reversion to barbarism has occurred in others. Some countries have seen the use of systematic sexual violence against women as a weapon of war to degrade and humiliate entire populations. Rape is the most despicable crime against women; mass rape is an abomination ... The eradication of such criminal forms of warfare is high on the Agenda for Peace of the United Nations."

UN Secretary-General Boutros Boutros-Ghali, on International Women's Day, 1993

The particular tragedies of women within the larger horrors of Bosnia-Herzegovina since 1992 and Rwanda in 1994 have been a powerful reminder of how vulnerable women and their families are when war breaks out. They have also demonstrated that the deliberate violation of the human rights of women is a central component of military strategy in all parts of the world. Governments, who in December 1993 adopted the Declaration on the Elimination of Violence against Women, are responsible for appalling levels of violence against women.

Responsibility for abuses against women goes beyond governments. The growth of nationalist, secessionist and ethnic conflicts which threaten all regions of the world with violence and bloodshed has seen armed opposition groups adopt similar methods of repression and terror in pursuit of their goals. Women have been killed, raped, ill-treated or taken hostage by armed opposition groups in all regions of the world.

Women are in double jeopardy. Discriminated against as women, they are also as likely as men, if not more so, to become victims of human rights violations. Few countries treat their women as well as their men. Despite moves to introduce equality for women on the legislative and political front, discrimination on grounds of gender remains an international reality. An Inter-Parliamentary Union Survey of 96 national parliaments, published in 1991, found that just 11 per cent of their members were women. While women are under-represented in national and international decision-making structures, they are over-represented among the victims of rights abuse.

Discrimination is a deadly disease. More women and girl-children die each day from various forms of gender-based discrimination and violence than from any other type of human rights abuse. Every year, according to the UN Children's Fund (UNICEF), more than a million infant girls die because they are born female. Every year, because of discrimination, millions of women are mutilated, battered to death, burned alive, stripped of their legal rights, and bought and sold in an unacknowledged but international trade in slaves for domestic or sexual purposes. Because of their gender women are at risk of a range of violent abuses by private organizations and individuals.

Universal and indivisible

The UN Declaration prohibiting violence against women calls for "the universal application to women of the rights and principles with regard to equality, security, liberty, integrity and dignity of all human persons". All governments are morally obliged to uphold this Declaration. They are also legally bound by international human rights treaties not to violate the fundamental human rights of their citizens. Many governments breach these treaties with impunity, some even reject the basic principle that human rights standards are universal standards which apply at all times in all situations and contexts.

The universality of human rights is being undermined by governments who argue that human rights must be subject to the interests of national security, economic strategy and local traditions. When it comes to women's human rights, many governments take a particularly restrictive view.

The issue of a government's "right" to interpret human rights according to its own philosophy or circumstances has emerged in the preparatory process for the Fourth UN World Conference on Women, to be held in the Chinese capital Beijing in September 1995. The first of a series of regional preparatory meetings for the conference took place in Jakarta, Indonesia, in June 1994. The Jakarta Declaration, although it upholds the universality and indivisibility of women's human rights, supports "the national competence of all countries to formulate, adopt and implement their respective policies on the advancement of women, mindful of their cultures, values and traditions, as well as their social, economic and political conditions".

This qualification is a powerful signal to the international human rights movement that asserting the universality of human rights may pose a formidable challenge in the run-up to the UN World Conference on Women. Anyone in doubt over whether the priorities of a particular government should take precedence over the collective will of the international community should ask themselves one simple question: what does the victim think? Would the woman who is raped and murdered in Indonesia for standing up for workers' rights consider this is a justifiable price to pay for a nation's "right" to interpret human rights according to local economic conditions? Does the woman who is flogged in Sudan for wearing trousers feel that this is a culturally acceptable punishment? Individual governments do not have the authority to define what constitutes a fundamental human right or who may enjoy that right.

Women's rights are human rights and human rights are not only universal, they are also indivisible. A woman who is arbitrarily detained, tortured, killed, made to "disappear" or jailed after an unfair trial has no chance of exercising her social, economic and cultural rights. Women who work to promote development, equality and other internationally recognized rights, in many countries, often face such grave threats to their civil and political rights that claiming their social, economic and cultural rights is impossible. Without respect for women's fundamental human rights, the themes of the UN World Conference on Women — women's rights to peace, equality and development — are unattainable.

*A woman forced to flee her home in the East Rand township of Thokoza, South Africa, in August 1993. Women and their dependent children make up most of the world's refugees and displaced people. Many of those forced to flee from war and conflict have become displaced; they are effectively refugees in their own countries. © Ken Oosterbroek/*The Star

A Guatemalan girl in the El Porvenir Refugee Camp in Chiapas, Mexico. By the beginning of 1994 the UN *High Commissioner for Refugees estimated that the total number of refugees worldwide was almost 20 million. Many of the countries where large refugee populations sought protection are among the world's poorest. © Howard J. Davies*

Challenges for human rights activists

The occasion of the UN Conference on Women offers both a focal point for campaigning on women's human rights in general and an opportunity to press governments attending the conference to guarantee that women's human rights are placed at the very heart of that meeting and the actions it takes. It is the task of the international human rights movement to ensure that all the human rights of women — civil and political, as well as social, economic and cultural — are upheld.

We want governments not simply to give their assent to the need to protect and promote women's human rights in yet another piece of paper. If it is to achieve anything, the conference must be more than just another occasion for fine rhetoric and conviviality. It must be a genuine catalyst for action and the swift delivery of real protection.

One of the most important goals in the campaign for women's human rights is to win concrete support for the principle that human rights are universal and indivisible. The international human rights movement faces other challenges. It must ensure that its message — human rights are women's right — is available to all, and crucially to women who have not enjoyed the right to education. Rates of illiteracy are far higher among women than men. It must ensure that women's human rights are respected and advanced within its own ranks and integrated in its research and its campaigns. Above all, the international human rights movement must develop preventive techniques and actions which could help stop violations of women's human rights.

Most of the advances which women have made towards claiming their rights have been the result of grass-roots campaigning, usually by independent women's rights organizations. If it is serious about preventing human rights violations against women, the international human rights movement must work in partnership with these organizations, and contribute to the worldwide campaign for women's human rights from its own area of expertise.

Violence against women

The UN Declaration on the Elimination of Violence against Women defines "violence against women" as encompassing, in addition to violence perpetrated by the state, physical, sexual and psychological violence in the family, including battering, sexual abuse of female children in the household, dowry-related violence, marital rape, female genital mutilation and other traditional practices harmful to women, non-spousal violence and violence related to exploitation; physical, sexual and psychological violence occurring within the general community, including rape, sexual abuse, sexual harassment and intimidation at work, in educational institutions and elsewhere, trafficking in women and forced prostitution.

The extent and severity of such practices must be recognized if we are fully to address the context in which human rights violations against women occur.

Domestic violence, for example, is an international problem. In most of the world's countries domestic violence is the cause of most violent attacks on women. In many countries it remains the main source of violence against women, even when prohibited by law. In several countries, men have the right to beat their wives, in many

A peasant woman of the Dai ethnic minority in Yunnan province, China, sentenced to death for drug-trafficking. She is being allowed to see her husband for the last time. She sits with her baby son on her knee, peeling him an orange, while her husband looks on from behind the police line. She was shot shortly afterwards. There is no evidence that the death penalty is a deterrent to drug-trafficking. There is plenty of evidence that most of those arrested, sentenced to death and executed for drug-trafficking are minor actors in the drug trade. **© Next, *Hong Kong***

they may do so without fear of punishment. In countless other countries, domestic violence is not treated seriously. The problem of domestic violence crosses borders, cultures and classes.

Domestic violence in the context of dowry disputes is a particularly serious problem in India, especially in the north of the country. Dowry deaths are also reported among immigrant communities outside India, in the United Kingdom, for example. The legislation dealing with the protection of women's rights in India is extensive. However, there is a huge gap between women's rights in law and women's practical experience. Official statistics make shocking reading. In 1992 the number of reported "dowry deaths" was 4,785; in 1993 some 5,000 women were reported to have died as a result of disputes involving dowries.

As a result of female genital mutilation, an estimated 110 million women suffer serious, even life-threatening, injuries throughout their adult lives. Female genital mutilation is a traditional practice which many of these women underwent as teenagers or children, some even as infants. The scale of the practice is enormous; around two million girls are mutilated every year (see Appendix).

Female genital mutilation occurs in some 20 countries in Africa, parts of Asia and the Middle East, and in immigrant communities in other regions, for example, Europe. For many years now, African women have been in the forefront of the campaign to eradicate female genital mutilation. Participants from 20 African countries, as well as representatives of international organizations, attending a 1984 seminar in Dakar on "Traditional Practices Affecting the Health of Women and Children" recommended that the practice be abolished and that "in order to change existing attitudes and practice, strong education programmes should be developed and carried out on a constant basis".

Thousands of women and girl-children have fallen victim to the trade in sexual and domestic slaves. This international industry exists with the knowledge and sometimes acquiescence of governments in whose countries it takes place. Reports of trafficking in women and girl-children have come from a number of countries, including Brazil, Myanmar (Burma), Sudan and Thailand. In China, trafficking in women as brides or as slave labour in the rural areas has been reported in recent years. During 1993, according to the Chinese Ministry of Public Security, police handled 15,000 cases of the sale of women or children.[1]

In numerous countries, it is activists against the many abuses encompassed by the Declaration who have been threatened, imprisoned, tortured, made to "disappear" and killed by agents of the same governments who in Geneva, New York or Vienna agree fine-sounding prohibitions of such actions. Governments must be held to their obligations if this international standard is not to become one more double standard.

Campaigning for women's human rights

This report is one of Amnesty International's contributions to worldwide campaigning for women's human rights, which in 1995 will have its focal point at the UN World Conference on Women. The report highlights many aspects of the work which must be done if we are indeed to have "Equality by the Year 2000" — the UN's objective. The report focuses on the vulnerability of women when war breaks out, and the role women have played in promoting human rights and campaigning for the victims of violations. It also examines situations in which women are at particular risk of human rights abuse.

Amnesty International's goal is to contribute to the observance throughout the world of the human rights set out in the Universal Declaration of Human Rights (UDHR). In pursuing this goal Amnesty International works to promote in general all the human rights enshrined in the UDHR and other international standards, through human rights education programs and campaigning for ratification of human rights treaties. At a minimum, the UDHR obliges governments to eradicate practices which are abusive and discriminatory of women. Few governments have taken this fundamental duty seriously.

Amnesty International's specific mandate for action is to oppose a set of grave violations of the rights to freedom of expression and freedom from discrimination, and of the right to physical and mental integrity. In particular, Amnesty International opposes arbitrary detention on political grounds, believing that no one should be imprisoned as a prisoner of conscience[2] and that no political prisoner should be imprisoned without a prompt and fair trial. Amnesty International also takes action to oppose torture, the death penalty, extrajudicial executions and other forms of arbitrary killing, and "disappearances". This report documents the global extent

Workers on strike at the* PT *Sumito, Sidaorjo East Java, in 1993. Factory workers suffer terrible exploitation in Indonesia where women take home on average half the male wage. Despite heavy restrictions on the right to strike and organize, Indonesia has seen a rising tide of industrial unrest in recent years.

and often systematic perpetration of these violations against women.

Amnesty International believes that governments are not only obliged not to violate women's human rights; they are obliged to promote and protect those rights. We campaign for governments to ratify the Convention on the Elimination of All Forms of Discrimination against Women and the International Covenant on Economic, Social and Cultural Rights as well as the International Covenant on Civil and Political Rights (ICCPR).

Amnesty International acknowledges the extent and gravity of abuses against women such as domestic violence, genital mutilation, forced prostitution and other violent acts committed by private individuals and organizations. Amnesty International also acknowledges the important work by individuals and other organizations against such abuses. However, Amnesty International's mandate for action is directed at governments and armed political groups, not private individuals and organizations and therefore does not include such abuses.

We also urge governments who are seriously committed to ending discrimination and violence against women (in both the public and private spheres), to adopt and fund comprehensive policies for widespread education and consciousness-raising about all women's human rights issues. When governments knowingly tolerate abuses such as domestic violence, female genital mutilation or trafficking in sexual slaves, as several do, the gap between what is public and what is private narrows.

A way forward

In adopting the 1993 Declaration prohibiting violence against women, the UN General Assembly welcomed "the role that women's movements have played in drawing increasing attention to the nature, severity and magnitude of the problem of violence against women".

The past two decades have seen women's organizations spring up around the world. Some work for their "disappeared" relatives; some are community activists, fighting for basic rights such as freedom from want; some are lawyers seeking justice for the unrepresented; some campaign against torture, some against domestic violence, some for equal treatment at work or for land rights and access to credit.

This wave of courage, creativity and commitment has all too often met a wall of government indifference and sometimes government repression of the cruellest kind. Few governments recognize the work of women's human rights organizations as a legitimate exercise of fundamental civil and political rights.

In 1993 the UN unequivocally stated that women's rights were human rights. The Declaration of the UN World Conference on Human Rights held in Vienna in June 1993 states: "The human rights of women and of the girl-child are an inalienable, integral and indivisible part of universal human rights." With the encouragement of the Conference the UN Commission on Human Rights appointed, in March 1994, a UN Special Rapporteur on violence against women. A few months after the conference, in December 1993, the UN adopted the Declaration on the Elimination of Violence against Women.

Yet the UN resolution to hold this conference, the first on human rights in 25 years, had made no mention of women, or of gender-based abuses. What made the difference, and forced women's human rights on to the agenda in Vienna, was the collective action of women in the years and months leading up to the conference.

The UN World Conference on Human Rights in Vienna in June 1993. Activists ensured that women's rights remained high on the agenda at the Conference. The Vienna Declaration adopted by the Conference stated that "The World Conference on Human Rights urges the full and equal enjoyment by women of all human rights and that this be a priority for Governments and for the UN." © Richard Reoch

As one activist put it: "The Conference [on Human Rights] was part of a continuing process to improve women's rights, which is precisely why women targeted it as an important place to be present and to be heard. And we were."[3]

Women's voices can be heard all over the world: demanding justice, protesting against discrimination, claiming rights, mourning dead husbands and comforting raped daughters. The job of the human rights movement is to make governments listen and ensure that they take action to protect and promote women's human rights.

ڤيتا
صنع تركيا
سمن نباتي
مهدرج نقي ١٠٠٪

1

Women and war

Left*: A Kurdish woman breaks solid sugar in a disused anti-tank mine case in Penjwin, Iraqi Kurdistan. No aspect of life has remained untouched by the Iraqi Government's policy of mass extermination of Kurds in recent years. Hundreds of thousands of Kurdish civilians have "disappeared" or been slaughtered by the Iraqi Government since mid-1988.*
© Brenda Prince/FORMAT

The spoils of war

A woman in the final stages of labour is attended by a hospital doctor. But this is Rwanda, the woman is a Tutsi, and the doctor — a Hutu — does not tend her, he slashes her to death with a long knife. He has rampaged through Kibuye hospital together with another doctor, finishing off the sick and injured.

The horror started just 11 days earlier, on 7 April 1994, the day after the presidents of Rwanda and Burundi were killed when their plane was shot down. A meeting was held for the members of Kibuye town's *Interahamwe* — the militia armed and organized by the former President and his party. Similar meetings were held throughout Rwanda: meetings to plan genocide.

Within hours parts of Kibuye town were ablaze, and the homes of members of the Tutsi ethnic minority group began to be systematically destroyed. Members of *Interahamwe*, the police and local government officials roamed through Kibuye over the following days, burning houses and killing. Women found sheltering in the parish church were raped, then pieces of wood were thrust into their vaginas, and they were left to die slowly. Tutsi sheltering in churches and municipal buildings were herded into Kibuye stadium. More than 15,000 people were crammed into the stadium. The prefect fired the first shots into the crowded arena. Then young and old alike were shot dead or hacked to death with machetes. Tear-gas canisters were thrown to flush out any survivors.

The scale, speed and brutality of the conflict in Rwanda shocked the world. As the history of the carnage emerged, it became clear that this was not some spontaneous upsurge of brutality, but calculated and organized genocide. Not all the killers were men: women were also caught up in the frenzy. But women who had played no part in the decision-making or the cruelty were tortured and killed.

Political murder, rape and torture are not unique to Rwanda. The end of the previous world power balance has contributed to the destabilization of entire countries and the eruption of new conflicts. Economic hardship exacerbates the struggle for resources and, when nation states are unable to deliver expectations, ethnic and religious differences come to the fore.

In such a fragmented and volatile world, all human rights are under threat. During conflicts — whether international wars, civil wars, or low-intensity insurgencies — the human rights of non-combatants are invariably at risk. Torture, massacres, "disappearances" become mere tactics; human rights are secondary to military advantage. Women suffer especially. They are caught up in conflicts largely not of their making. They become the butt of reprisal killings. They make up most of the world's refugees and displaced people. They are left to rear families by themselves. They are raped and sexually abused with impunity.

Rape: a weapon of war

Rape by soldiers of vanquished women has a long history. The Crusaders in the 12th century raped women in the name of religion. In the 15th century the so-called conquest of the Americas saw the mass rape of indigenous women by the invading forces. English soldiers in the 18th century systematically raped Scottish women during the subjugation of Scotland. Rape was a weapon of terror used by the German army in the First World War, a weapon of revenge used by the Soviet army in the Second World War.

Half a century ago, rape in war was outlawed by the Geneva Conventions which state: "Women shall be especially protected ... against rape, enforced prostitution, or any form of indecent assault." Rape may be outlawed under the international rules governing conflicts, but women are being raped — terrorized, degraded and violated — in every modern conflict on the planet. Women are raped because their bodies are seen as the legitimate spoils of war. Rape by combatants is an act of torture, and clearly prohibited by the rules of war and by international human rights law. Yet few governments or armed opposition groups have taken action to prevent rape during conflict.

Rape by the armed forces in Bosnia-Herzegovina has received

Women of Kunan Poshpora village, Jammu and Kashmir. In February 1991 at least 23 women were reportedly raped at gunpoint in their homes when soldiers raided the village. Some were said to have been gang-raped, others to have been raped in front of their children. The youngest victim was 13, the oldest was 80. © Anthony Woods

unprecedented publicity and the extent of sexual abuse there has caused shock and dismay. Women have been raped in their homes by soldiers from their own town or strangers passing through. Women prisoners have been raped by soldiers and guards in detention centres. Women have been raped in an organized and systematic way: they have been imprisoned in hotels and other buildings specifically so that they could be raped by soldiers.

In one such case, a 17-year-old Muslim girl was taken by Serbs from her village to huts in woods near by in June 1992. She was held there for three months, along with 23 other women. She was among 12 women who were raped repeatedly in the hut in front of the other women — when they tried to defend her they were beaten off by the soldiers.

Soldiers from all sides in the conflict have become rapists and women from all backgrounds have been victims. However, most of the victims have been Muslim women raped by Serbian soldiers and irregulars. The sexual abuse of women has been part of a wider pattern of warfare, characterized by intimidation and abuse of Muslims and Croats which have led thousands to flee or be expelled from their home areas. The UN Special Rapporteur on the conflict in the former Yugoslavia reported:

> "*... rape was being used as an instrument of ethnic cleansing ... There are reliable reports of public rapes, for example, in front of a whole village, designed to terrorize the population and force ethnic groups to flee.*"[4]

It is extremely difficult to assess the full extent of the sexual abuse of women in Bosnia-Herzegovina. The shame and social stigma attached discourage many women from reporting what has been done to them. Some obliterate the experience from their conscious memory because recalling the trauma is unbearably painful. The administrative chaos that has accompanied armed conflict in Bosnia-Herzegovina has rendered the systematic collection of data very difficult. In addition, rape has been widely used as a propaganda weapon, with all sides minimizing or denying the abuses committed by their own forces and maximizing those of their opponents.

The difficulties of assessing the evidence do not hide the fact that in Bosnia-Herzegovina the military have used rape to dehumanize their opponents in the minds of their own soldiers, to undermine and punish their enemies and to reward their troops. As a result, women have been raped not only by strangers but also by people who were once their neighbours.

Croatian forces raided a house in Novi Grad in which a group of Serbian women were sheltering in June 1992. Four of the women were seized and taken to the house of their Croatian neighbours, who had accused them of harbouring Serbian fighters. Fifteen men, from a force known as the Fire Horses, were waiting. For the next five hours they gang-raped the women. The Fire Horses reportedly came from Posavska Mahala and surrounding villages and were cited in other reports of rape.

Rape and abuse of women have been reported in almost every modern situation of armed conflict, whether internal or international in nature. Kuwaiti women and foreign domestic servants in Kuwait were subjected to sexual violence from the Iraqi invaders. Women in Peru have been subjected to brutal violence by both parties to the long-running conflict in that country: women have been raped by men from both sides. Women in Liberia have been raped in the course of a civil war that has torn the country apart and has continued sporadically throughout the 1990s. In Papua

New Guinea, a girl from South Bougainville was raped in public by a government soldier in September 1993.

In East Timor, the former Portuguese colony which Indonesia has occupied illegally, in defiance of UN resolutions, since 1975, sexual abuse and rape have been widely reported. One woman and her family were tortured for several days by members of the military in Baucau who were looking for her 22-year-old son, a suspected independence activist. The woman, a 50-year-old widow from Baucau, was arrested on 8 September 1992 and interrogated about her son's whereabouts. When she denied knowing where he was, she was stripped naked, beaten and kicked and given electric shocks. Three days after her arrest, one of her nephews and her unmarried sister-in-law were called in for questioning. They too were interrogated under torture; her sister-in-law was also sexually abused. A 25-year-old student from Quelicai was repeatedly raped by a military officer in Baucau, following her arrest on 20 December 1992. Subsequently released, she is believed to have become pregnant as a result of the rape.

Women in the Indian state of Jammu and Kashmir are reluctant to report rape. Unmarried women fear that they will be unable to marry, while for married women, being a rape victim can mean their husbands will leave them. There is strong evidence that members of the Indian security forces have used rape as a tactic in an increasingly violent suppression of the campaign for Kashmiri independence.

Around midnight on 10 October 1992, an Indian army unit raided the village of Chak Saidapora, near Shopian. They carried out a house-to-house search, in the course of which at least six women were raped. Among them were a woman of 60 and an 11-year-old girl called Ziatoon.

That incident was just one in a continuing pattern. Over a year later, on 22 November 1993, Indian soldiers entered the village of Warapora. Sara, a young woman, was out collecting firewood. Eye-witnesses saw five soldiers approaching her. They found her dead body later that day. Her clothes had been torn off and the post-mortem revealed "... marks of violence on neck, breasts, left knee ... and extensive vaginal tear". The Indian Government has denied many allegations of rape by its forces, claiming that they are "trumped up ... to malign the reputation of the security forces".

In Haiti, where the military government that ousted the elected president Jean-Bertrand Aristide clung to power until September

1994, the number of cases of rape by the official security forces and their civilian auxiliaries had risen in the first nine months of the year. Many of the victims have been women living in poor urban neighbourhoods and rural villages, where support for President Aristide was strongest. In a typical case, about 15 members of an armed civilian militia burst into the home of one of President Aristide's supporters in the capital, Port-au-Prince, on 15 April 1994. He was not there but they interrogated his father before killing him in cold blood. Several of them then raped the only other person in the house — the activist's sister, who was just 14 years old.

In Djibouti, in the Horn of Africa, government troops have been fighting armed opponents in the north and southwest of the country from the Front for the Restoration of Unity and Democracy (FRUD). The FRUD draws its support mainly from the Afar ethnic group. Between 3 and 10 March 1994, at least a dozen Afar girls and women were raped by government soldiers in the north of the country. One of the victims had been previously raped by government soldiers in January.

Beyond the brutality and trauma of the rape itself, which often causes life-long psychological damage to the victim, sexual assault can result in serious physical injury, forced pregnancy, disease and even death.

Rape is not an accident of war, or an incidental adjunct to armed conflict. Its widespread use in times of conflict reflects the special terror it holds for women, the special power it gives the rapist over his victim, the special contempt it displays for its victims. The use of rape in conflict reflects the inequalities women face in their everyday lives in peacetime. Until governments live up to their obligations to ensure equality, and end discrimination against women, rape will continue to be a favourite weapon of the aggressor.

The flight from terror

Between 1981 and 1993 the number of refugees worldwide doubled from eight million to more than 20 million; millions more are displaced within their own countries. In most cases they have been forced to flee situations of war or civil strife.

More than 80 per cent of refugees are women and children. "There is no doubt that refugee women, particularly those on their own, are more vulnerable to exploitation and deprivation of rights, at every stage of flight, than are refugee men," according to

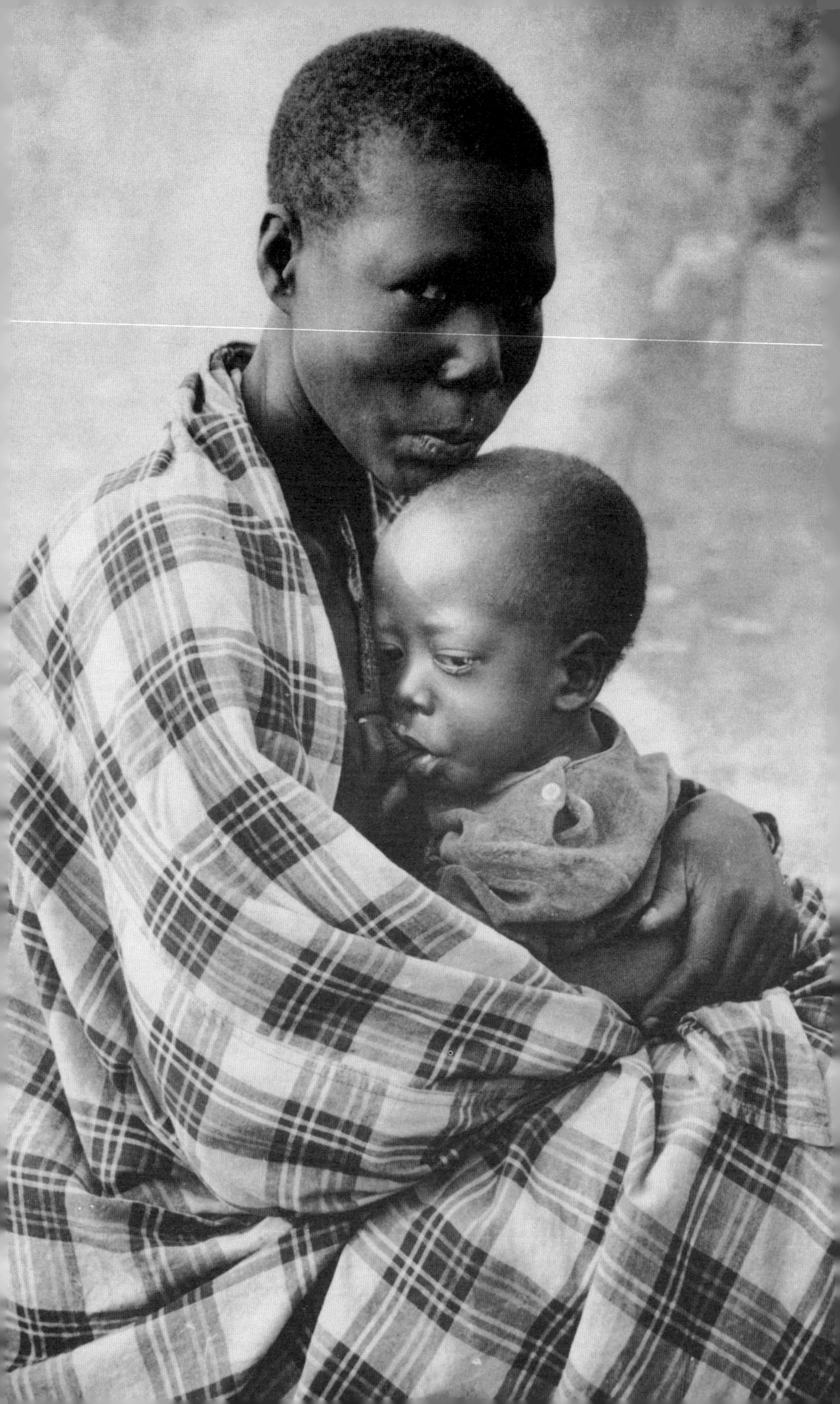

Ann Howarth-Wiles, UNHCR Senior Coordinator for Refugee Women, despite "the exceptional resilience and resourcefulness of refugee women and their ability to cope with tremendous hardship".[5]

Refugee women and girl-children are particularly vulnerable to sexual abuse. So serious is the problem that the UNHCR has issued guidelines for officials working with refugees, identifying measures to be taken to protect refugee women against sexual violence.

Refugee women are particularly vulnerable during flight, when they may be attacked by pirates, bandits, members of the security forces, locals, smugglers, or other refugees. Border guards have detained women and girls for weeks to exploit them sexually. Smugglers sometimes assist female refugees across the border in exchange for sex or money. A refugee woman fleeing the Mengistu Government in Ethiopia described her journey to a neighbouring country:

> *"We were four people: my two children, four and two years old, our guide and myself. I was five months pregnant. On our way we were stopped by two men who asked us where we were going. When we explained, one pulled me aside and said: 'No safe passage before sex!' ... he forced me down, kicked me in the stomach and raped me in front of my children. He knew I was pregnant, but that made no difference to him."*

Nor are women safe when they arrive in the country of asylum. A Haitian woman seeking asylum in the USA was reported to have been raped by an Immigration and Naturalization Service guard while held in a Florida detention centre in early 1991. After the assault she suffered from severe depression, including inability to eat, "nightmares and flashes".

Women confined in refugee camps, sometimes for years, are at risk of sexual violence from officials and from male refugees. Unaccompanied women and girls are the most vulnerable and in

---

Page 23: Somali nomads, displaced by the famine and civil war, at the "Italian Village", a displaced people's camp outside Bardera in southern Somalia. Hardship and deprivation face women who have lost their homes, their possessions, their friends and their roots as they search for safety. © Howard J Davies

Page 24: ***A Rwandan mother comforts her child. Women who have taken no part in conflicts have to endure the loneliness and vulnerability of separation and bereavement. © Jenny Matthews***

some situations have been regarded as common sexual property by guards and male refugees alike. Forced prostitution also occurs, with officials collaborating with local prostitution rings to share the profits. In camps where men control the distribution of food, women may be coerced into sexual acts by men in exchange for essential documents or rations. When women are applying for asylum, officials may demand sex in return for refugee status.

Nearly a quarter of Somalia's six million people fled the brutal civil war which erupted in 1991 and ravaged the country for two years, but not all found safe refuge.

Some 300,000 Somali refugees went to Kenya, where they shelter in camps in the North Eastern Province. Hundreds of Somali women have been raped in these camps. The Kenya Chapter of the International Federation of Women Lawyers (FIDA) employs a woman lawyer to take up cases of Somali women who have been raped in the camps in Garissa and Wajir. According to FIDA, the incidence of rape had not reduced during 1994.

International law prohibits the forcible return of refugees to countries where their lives or freedom are in danger. But many governments assert that asylum-seekers are simply looking for a better standard of living in more affluent countries. So while accepting the principle that no one should be forcibly returned to a country where their lives or liberty are at risk, many governments limit its application. Some of the world's wealthiest countries apply a restrictive interpretation of the international definition of a refugee entitled to protection.

Many governments also impose visa requirements and apply detention policies which can obstruct asylum-seekers or deter them from entering the country where they wish to seek protection. Sometimes people are prevented from boarding planes to leave their country because they do not have visas. And in an increasing number of countries, substantial financial penalties, in some cases amounting to thousands of dollars per person, are imposed on airlines who carry passengers, including asylum-seekers, who do not have the required travel documents or visas.

In recent years states, particularly those in Europe which are members of the European Union (EU), have been developing coordination of their asylum policies in ways which make it difficult for asylum-seekers to get a fair hearing. The measures taken include the introduction of the concepts of "safe countries of origin" and "safe countries of asylum". Increasingly, asylum-seekers can be

Demonstration in Bonn, Germany, on 26 May 1993, against an amendment to the German Constitution and a new asylum law which placed restrictions on asylum-seekers. The banner reads: "No wall around Europe. Permanent right to stay for all."* © *Rex Features

turned away without a proper review because they come from countries considered "safe".

Although women are the majority of refugees, they are a minority of those who succeed in gaining asylum in the wealthy countries of the North. Often those hearing asylum applications fail to categorize violations of women's rights as persecution. The asylum process itself, which requires applicants to tell strangers in uniform what has happened to them — often repeatedly — works against women victims of rape and sexual abuse. Many are too ashamed or traumatized to tell their stories, especially to men.

The vast majority of women who flee in search of safety never get as far as seeking asylum abroad. According to the UN, there are more than 100 million displaced people worldwide, some 80 per cent of whom are women and dependent children. In their desperate search for safety, these women have effectively become refugees within their own countries, struggling to survive far from their own homes.

Hundreds of thousands of black South Africans were forced to leave their homes and communities as a result of the widespread political violence which racked South Africa in the years before the

An elderly woman displaced by the conflict in Colombia. The army and army-backed paramilitary forces have sown terror in the countryside for more than a decade. Tens of thousands of people have fled from their villages to the shanty towns of Colombia's cities, where they face grinding poverty and further violence. © Jenny Matthews

country's first democratic elections in April 1994. Whole communities were torn apart by the violence as families and individuals were targeted because of their real or suspected political affiliation or ethnic identity. The security forces, far from providing effective protection to those vulnerable to attack, actively colluded with one of the factions in the conflict.

In the province of KwaZulu-Natal, scene of some of the most intense conflict in recent years, the April 1994 elections did not see an end to the violence. People are still being killed and maimed and having their homes destroyed. It has been estimated that between 800,000 and one million people have been displaced in KwaZulu-Natal since the late 1980s. Because of the fear of further attack, those fleeing their homes did not stay in demarcated refugee camps; many were forced to take temporary refuge in churches, halls, police stations, sugarcane fields or with friends and relatives.

The victims of violent dispossession suffer immense trauma. Mrs Magwaza was one of a group of women who fled with their children to the sugarcane fields on 8 July 1994 when armed men attacked and burned their homes in Umlalazi, northern KwaZulu-Natal. Five days later, overwhelmed by her circumstances and her inability to provide for her children, Mrs Magwaza hanged herself.

The failure of the police to investigate reported attacks and to bring the perpetrators to justice has contributed to some women being repeatedly displaced. Mrs Ntuli (not her real name) was first forced to flee from her home in the KwaMondi area in September 1991. She and her young baby took refuge in a nearby forest. When she was able to return to her home she found it had been ransacked. Two years later, in 1993, she was again forced to flee with her family when armed men accompanied by police officers in an armoured vehicle came to her home. Mrs Ntuli and her family finally left the area after men opened fire on her aunt's house while she was there collecting her children after work. In February 1994 Mrs Ntuli's aunt was also forced to flee from her home after the same men attacked and burned her home. Both women had reported the attacks to the police and given them information about the identity of the attackers, but the police took no action.

In Colombia, where army-backed paramilitary squads have sown terror in the countryside for more than a decade, villagers face a stark choice. They can collaborate with the paramilitaries, abandon their farms and leave the area, or die. Paramilitary squads have overrun whole villages, taken control of the administration and exacted "taxes" from the population. They have killed, terrorized and driven out villagers and repopulated communities with their own supporters. Tens of thousands of people have fled from their villages to the shanty towns of Colombia's cities, where they face grinding poverty and further violence.

Casualties of conflict

> *"In a war the winner does not have to pay. Human rights have no priority in any war."*[6]
>
> Former Uruguayan general, talking of counter-insurgency operations in which he had been involved in the 1970s

Only five per cent of the casualties in the First World War were civilians. By the Second World War this figure had risen to 50 per cent. By the mid-1990s, about 80 per cent of the casualties in conflicts were civilians — most of them women and children.[7]

As the 20th century draws to a close, women who have taken no part in conflicts are being murdered, raped and mutilated. Others have to endure the loneliness and vulnerability of separation and bereavement. Hardship and deprivation face women who have to support a family alone, in an economy itself distorted by the violence. Millions of women have lost their homes, their possessions, their friends and their roots as they search for safety. Even women whose families are reunited after conflicts frequently face violence at the hands of men who have been brutalized by war.

A proliferation of situations of armed conflict is devastating women's lives in many quarters of the globe. Often, government forces face opposition from organizations which draw their support from a particular ethnic group which has been excluded from power and denied access to resources. In country after country, troops engaged in counter-insurgency operations have targeted

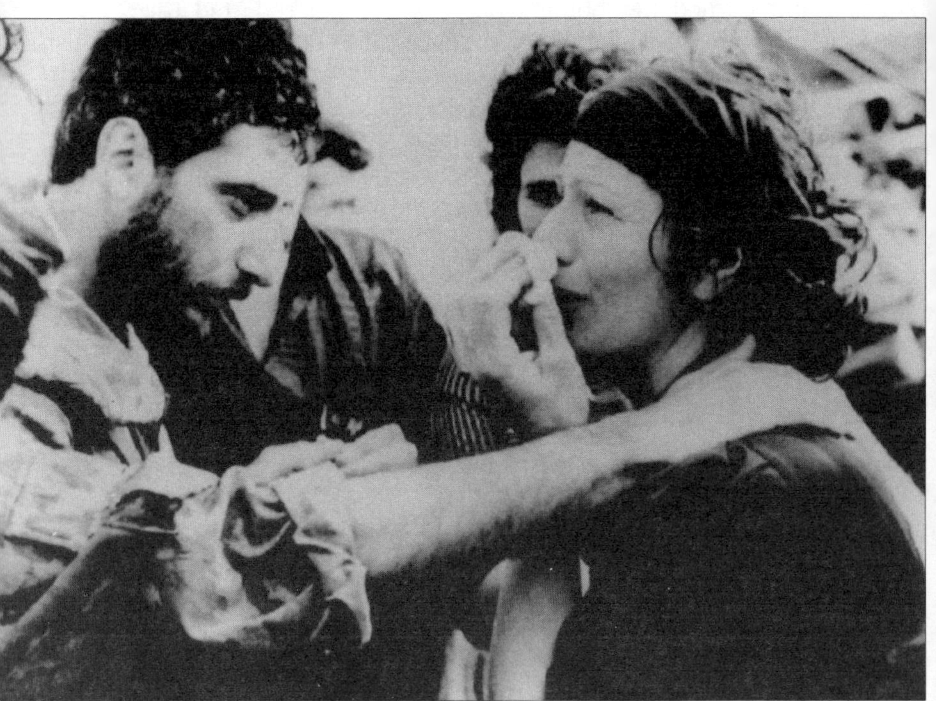

A Georgian refugee from Abkhazia who has just lost one of her sons in the fighting is comforted by a soldier on his way to the front. Human rights abuses have been committed by both sides in the bitter conflict over the disputed region of Abkhazia. © Associated Press

women just because they come from the ethnic group identified as "the enemy".

Indigenous women and men in the southeastern Mexican state of Chiapas have been victimized by the security forces and by powerful local landowners and their allies for decades. Bitter land disputes and allegations of electoral fraud have fuelled tensions, and the least powerful have suffered the most.

In January 1994 an armed indigenous peasant movement took control of several towns in Mexico, demanding land rights and electoral reforms. After several days of heavy fighting, they retired to the mountains. Since then, indigenous peoples have continued to suffer repeated threats and attacks by the Mexican security forces.

In Chiapas three sisters aged 16, 18 and 20 were returning to their village with their mother after selling their produce in a local town on 4 June 1994. The three young Tzeltal women were stopped by soldiers at a road-block, then taken off to a nearby building. There approximately 10 soldiers raped them. They were warned that they would be killed if they reported being raped. The women were so terrified that it was weeks before they told anyone what had happened. An independent medical examination supported their allegations.

In Mali, West Africa, women have been among scores of people killed in renewed ethnic conflict in mid-1994, despite a peace agreement signed in 1992. Opposition armed groups — mostly from Tuareg and Moorish ethnic minorities — have killed defenceless civilians, and the armed forces have extrajudicially executed civilians in reprisal. After two soldiers were killed in Ménaka on 20 April 1994, at least four civilians were shot dead in cold blood, apparently just because they were Tuareg, including a woman in her sixties. On 13 May Tuareg fighters reportedly killed several civilians in Gao, including the wife and children of Mohamed El Yéhia, and on 8 June a Moorish armed group killed a military guard, his wife and daughter in an attack on a prison in Niafunké. There are thousands of Tuareg and Moorish refugees in neighbouring countries, fearing to return home because of the continuing unrest. One of them, Salka Mint Makhfouze, witnessed the extrajudicial execution of her husband, Mohamed Ould Sidi Boubacar Cheick, on 26 June 1994 by commandos, apparently assisted by a vigilante group.

The nation state has all but collapsed in some parts of the

world, splintering into patchworks of territory controlled by competing warlords. Caught in the cross-fire, women from the poorest and most vulnerable sections of society have nowhere to turn. When the rule of law breaks down, there is no authority to protect the weak from the strong.

In Somalia hundreds of defenceless women were killed by rival political groups fighting a civil war which destroyed central government and fragmented the country. Thousands more died of starvation in a famine which grew out of the conflict.

The civil war began in early 1991, shortly after the overthrow of former President Mohamed Siad Barre's brutal 21-year dictatorship. Fighting was widespread as different armed groups, generally based on particular clans or sub-clans, disputed control of different areas. Women were raped and murdered solely because they belonged to an opposing clan.

For example, in April 1992, General Aideed's faction of the ruling United Somali Congress party massacred civilians in the town of Bulohawo, near Somalia's border with Kenya. A survivor recalled:

> *"I saw people with their tongues cut out or their arms or legs cut off, left to die. Women were gang-raped and bayonetted in the vagina. Pregnant women had their stomachs slit open."*

United States (US) and UN troops went into Somalia with a mandate to alleviate the widespread famine. A large proportion of the famine relief supplies brought into the country had been stolen at gunpoint by armed groups, some linked to clan-based political groups. But the humanitarian role of the UN and US troops was marred by their killing hundreds of unarmed Somali civilians in Mogadishu, including women on a protest demonstration. UN troops also failed to abide by the UN's own standards when they detained hundreds of Somalis without charge or trial and denied them the right to see their families and lawyers.

Somalia is not the only African country torn apart by internal conflicts. In both Liberia and neighbouring Sierra Leone, brutal civil wars have led to thousands of women and men being killed

---

Left: ***Refugees in Croatia feed pigeons while waiting for a train to safety. At the end of 1993 some 250,000 people were believed to remain displaced within Croatia. © Jenny Matthews***

not for anything they did, but because of their ethnic group, or where they lived. The patterns in the two countries have been similar. Women who live in areas recaptured from opposing forces who are identified as supporting the opposing forces have been summarily executed.

Afghanistan is another country ravaged by a conflict in which civilians, far from being protected by their non-combatant status, have been deliberately targeted and where women, far from being protected by their gender, have been attacked because of it. Continued fighting over control of territory results in the killing of countless civilians caught in cross-fire, including women and children. As territory changes hands after a long battle, an entire local population may become the target of retaliatory punishment, mainly torture and killings, by the new warlord if he decides that they had cooperated with the previous warlord. A warlord's fighters are usually rewarded by the property they loot or confiscate from the conquered population. This again usually involves massacre of the male members of the families and raping of the women.

In the first three months of 1994 more than 1,200 women, men and children were killed and at least 12,000 injured in the capital, Kabul. Both the government and the armed groups that control most of the country outside Kabul have used mass killings in their efforts to keep or gain power, attacking hungry crowds waiting for emergency food distribution and bombarding hospitals, mosques and churches.

Women working in professional jobs in government offices have also been targeted by Mujahideen groups which consider that education under the former regime has "poisoned" women's minds and turned them against Islamic principles. These women's offices and homes have been raided and several of them have been ill-treated and raped. Hundreds of professional women joined the mass exodus from Afghanistan. At least 200,000 people fled from Kabul in the first three months of 1994.

Generations of suffering

While many of the conflicts in which women's rights are abused have erupted in the 1990s, others have been going on for decades. Both military and civilian governments run counter-insurgency operations in which women are raped, tortured and killed. Human rights — supposedly protected by the whole weight of international law — are simply not a consideration.

This has been the experience of women living in the southeastern provinces of Turkey. Since the government announced in July 1993 that its armed forces would pursue a policy of "total conflict" against guerrillas of the Kurdish Workers' Party (PKK), human rights abuses against Kurdish villagers have been reported on a daily basis.

The country's southeastern provinces and their mainly Kurdish population are being subjected to a major military operation to crush the PKK and all manifestations of Kurdish separatism. The government, the police and armed forces, and the judicial system — the state prosecutors and the courts — are collaborating in the crack-down. Women have been seized, publicly humiliated, beaten, abducted, shot, raped and killed. Neither pregnant women, women with new-born babies, young girls nor the very old have been spared.

Villages throughout the southeast have been raided with the utmost ferocity by the security forces. More than 1,000 villages have reportedly been forcibly evacuated, swelling the population of the regional capital, Diyarbakir, from 450,000 in 1990 to one million in mid-1994.

A typical operation took place in July 1994 in villages in Diyarbakir province. After a clash with PKK guerrillas, the security forces began to forcibly evacuate the villages of Akçayurt (Kurdish name: Dernan), Kaladibi (Horsel), Saribudak (Melekan), outlying districts of Saklica (Hursik) and Yayladere (Zeleheydan), between Genç and Hani. They burned many houses and barns and destroyed irrigation pumps and crops. An estimated 2,000 evacuated villagers, including women and children, were herded into a containment area set up by the security forces adjacent to the Topçular Gendarmerie Post near Damlatepe and held for a week in cruel and inhuman conditions. Many were reported to have been severely tortured. Four women wearing clothes of red, yellow and green, the colours of Kurdish nationalism, were taken and tortured. They were later set free. Emine Çeliksöz of Yayladere village, who was pregnant, was reportedly left in labour for several hours in the burning sun while the security forces prevented other women from helping her. Children were beaten and kicked.

Some of the women, Mehmet Biçakçi, Ahmet Biçakçi, Hasan Biçakçi, and the daughters of the village *imam* (prayer leader), were kept for three days in the health centre while soldiers allegedly humiliated and sexually assaulted them.

Sisters Suzan Atsan and Zeliha Atsan were taken to the Çemel

Young girl wounded when Indonesian soldiers opened fire on a peaceful procession at the Santa Cruz cemetery in Dili, East Timor, in November 1991. Some 270 people were killed and another 200 "disappeared". © Steve Cox

stream just outside the containment area and repeatedly held under water over a period of approximately two hours, after which they had extreme difficulty in breathing, suffering violent coughing fits and fever. Zeynel Aydin, one of the villagers, told Amnesty International:

"There were about 2,000 villagers — including children. Over the seven days many people were tortured. The village children, Fatma [a four-year-old girl], Emine [a two-year-old girl] and Kasim [a four-year-old boy] were beaten by soldiers. The soldiers said to the young girls, 'If you want to escape from here, you will have to marry us'. They stripped several women naked and attacked them."

The newspaper *Hürriyet* reported that the villages had been burned by PKK guerrillas — a claim denied by the villagers. On 15 July the containment area began to be emptied. The families have since fled to other parts of Turkey.

The freedom of the press to report on such atrocities has been under constant attack from the government. The Kurdish-owned *Özgür Gündem* was almost the only newspaper which consistently reported on human rights violations in the south-east. During the first two years of its existence, six of the newspaper's journalists were killed in circumstances that suggest security force involvement. *Özgür Gündem* closed in 1994.

Journalist Aysel Malkaç went missing in Istanbul on 7 August 1993 after she left *Özgür Gündem*'s office. Eye-witnesses saw her being detained in the street by plainclothes police officers. During the week before her "disappearance", the newspaper's office and staff had been under heavy surveillance by the police, who had patrolled nearby streets and monitored the newspaper's telephone calls.

Ten members of the newspaper's Diyarbakir staff were arrested in January 1994. One was Necmiye Aslanoglu, who had been detained the previous November. After being released that time she said that she had been stripped of her clothes and beaten, dragged by the hair and suspended by the arms while she was given electric shocks through her navel and toes.

It is more and more difficult for the outside world to know what is happening to the women and men who live in the southeast of Turkey. Even the most courageous human rights activists have been forced to leave the southeast after constant intimidation, threats, and the murder of 10 members of the Human Rights Association (HRA). Only one of the 13 HRA branches in the area is working at full strength.

Civil war has divided Angola since independence in 1975. The Peace Accords agreed in 1991 by the government and UNITA, the National Union for the Total Independence of Angola, have been repeatedly undermined by human rights abuse and political violence on both sides. Linda Kalufele lived in Lobito with her husband Carlos and children. In early January 1993 she went to visit relatives in Huambo, a UNITA stronghold. Immediately after her return police came to arrest her, apparently on suspicion that she was a UNITA supporter. Her husband refused to let her go with the police alone and got into the vehicle with her. They both "disappeared". In the wake of government military advances, UNITA supporters, including women, have been extrajudicially executed. UNITA has committed thousands of deliberate and arbitrary killings as it has conquered territory. In July 1993 UNITA murdered seven people in Cabuta, Kwanza Sul province: a survivor said that the dead included four men who were beheaded, two women who were first raped, and a child. During 1994 there were further reports of both sides deliberately killing unarmed civilians. A new peace agreement was signed on 20 November 1994.

In Colombia thousands of women are numbered among the more than 20,000 people killed for political reasons since 1986 — most by the armed forces and their paramilitary protégés.

There are often no warnings before attacks on people living in areas where guerrilla forces are active. Women and men working hard to make a living as peasant farmers have been targeted by the security forces as potential guerrilla collaborators. Often the army has attempted to disguise cold-blooded murders as armed confrontation. Only exceptionally have the murderers been brought to justice; the vast majority of members of the armed forces responsible for gross human rights violations continue on active service.

On 5 October 1993 soldiers from the Palacé Battalion launched a counter-insurgency operation in the municipality of Riofrío, Valle de Cauca department. Thirteen people from the village of El Bosque were dragged from their homes, tortured and shot. Five women were raped. Military commanders immediately claimed the victims were members of an armed opposition group. The commander of the Palacé Battalion, Lieutenant-Colonel Luis Felipe Becerra Bohórquez, who arrived by helicopter shortly after the massacre, stated that the 13 people had died in a confrontation with his troops. However, it was soon established that in fact the victims were not guerrillas but peasant farmers.

The village of El Bosque was a well-organized community, strongly influenced by the church. The community has been devastated. The massacre left two babies and several other children orphaned, and at least 18 of the 22 families living in the village have fled. Their homes were ransacked and in mid-1994 they were still too frightened to return.

After the Riofrío massacre the government announced that Lieutenant-Colonel Becerra had been discharged from the army. However, his career provides a striking example of how impunity fosters further human rights violations. For the massacre in Riofrío was not the first by troops under his command; he had already been implicated in another massacre, that of 21 banana plantation workers in Urabá in 1988.

Several of the civilian judges who investigated the Urabá massacres received repeated death threats. As a result one left the country; her father was murdered shortly afterwards. Only days before leaving, she had issued arrest warrants against four army officers, including Luis Felipe Becerra, then a major, in connection with the killings. Luis Felipe Becerra was not arrested and the case never went to trial. Far from being disciplined, he was repeatedly promoted.

Disciplinary investigations of the massacre in Riofrío have focused on the attempts to conceal it. To this day, no one has been charged in connection with the murders and rapes in Riofrío.

In neighbouring Peru a similarly long and dirty war has been fought between the government and armed opposition groups, notably the Communist Party of Peru, widely known as Shining Path. At least 27,000 people have lost their lives in the insurgency, about half of them killed by government troops. Between 1983 and 1993 Amnesty International recorded details of more than 4,300 people who were taken into custody by the security forces and then "disappeared"; the true figure is believed to be far higher.

In the past two years a pattern has emerged in Peru in which thousands of women and men have been falsely imprisoned under wide-ranging and imprecise anti-terrorism laws which give the police virtually unlimited powers and severely limit the rights of the defence. Between May 1992 and July 1994, more than 7,000 people were detained on terrorism charges: many of them were tortured.

Esperanza Boy Bautista is one of the 7,000. She was detained by the army in July 1992, together with two of her young daughters. In mid-1994 Amnesty International interviewed her in Chiclayo Women's Prison, Lambayeque department, where she was awaiting trial on charges of "terrorism". She told Amnesty International that her father-in-law had accused her of being connected with terrorists because he wanted her husband to live with another woman. She also said her father-in-law had raped her. She described how she was forced to "confess":

> *"They beat me ... they submerged me in a drum of water ... they tied my arms behind me with a rope and they punished me. And my two children were crying ..."*

In Africa's largest country, Sudan, another ruthless government has used famine as a weapon in its efforts to crush the opposition to its rule in the south of the country. Its troops and militias have killed thousands of women, men and children from southern ethnic groups and deliberately destroyed their means of livelihood in the civil war fought since 1983.

During 1993 the army and an army-backed civilian militia attacked villages in the southern provinces, torturing and killing

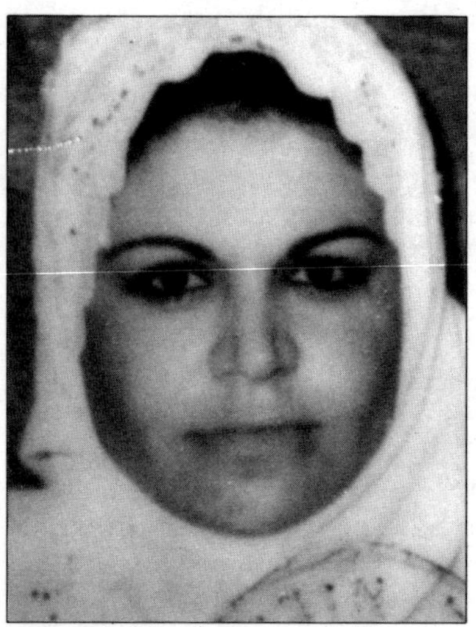

Najah Abu Dalal was shot by Israeli forces while standing in her courtyard in Nusayrat refugee camp in the Gaza Strip on 21 April 1993. She died five days later.

women and men, as well as killing livestock and burning crops. In March 1993, for example, militiamen attacked villages around the railway line in Bahr al-Ghazal. They raped scores of women, murdered villagers and abducted more than 300 women and children, most of whom were sold into slavery. Many of the women were taken as concubines.

In the West Bank and Gaza Strip, occupied by Israel since 1967, an alarming number of women and children have been shot dead by Israeli soldiers. Before the present peace process, Israeli efforts to crush the Palestinian uprising which began in December 1987 resulted in the deaths of more than 1,000 Palestinians. Many were killed during clashes with the army or border police. Some died as a result of beatings or torture, or after the misuse of tear-gas. Many — like Najah Abu Dalal — were just going about their everyday lives.

Najah Abu Dalal was standing in her family courtyard talking to a relative on 21 April 1993, when she fell to the ground, mortally wounded. She had been shot in the left eye, apparently by a soldier stationed at the top of a house some 100 metres away. The ambulance that took her to hospital was, according to a relative who went with her, held up by soldiers for 15 vital minutes. She died five days later. The Israeli authorities have so far failed to carry out an adequate investigation into her death.

Thiagarajah Selvanithy, a Sri Lankan student, was dragged from her home by Liberation Tigers of Tamil Eelam (LTTE) militants in August 1991. She has not been seen since.

'Caught between two fires': abuses by armed political groups

"Two people arrived at my home, a woman and a man, but I didn't know they were from Shining Path, they were dressed in ordinary clothes. I gave them something to eat ... Yes, I fed them, we're in the habit of giving help to our fellow creatures ..."

These are the words of Juana Valderrama Vargas, a Peruvian peasant woman in jail accused of terrorist offences interviewed by Amnesty International in 1994. She is illiterate, has no lawyer, and her husband and three sons are also in prison on similar charges.

Millions of women are caught between the government and an armed opposition, both of which use violence in pursuit of their goals. For the victims of abductions, torture and summary executions, the pain and suffering are the same, regardless of who is responsible. Armed opposition groups all over the world have resorted to such brutal tactics against innocent bystanders. Women have not been spared.

Thiagarajah Selvanithy

(known as Selvi) is a prisoner. She is not held in a prison run by the Government of Sri Lanka, where she lives. Selvi is being held by the Liberation Tigers of Tamil Eelam (LTTE), an armed group fighting for a separate Tamil state in the northeast of Sri Lanka.

Selvi was a drama and theatre student at the University of Jaffna, in her final year when she was dragged from her home by LTTE militants in August 1991. She was active in women's groups and had once been a member of the women's wing of a rival Tamil group.

According to some estimates, the LTTE holds more than 2,000 people. These include Tamils suspected of being government informers, people who have criticized LTTE policies, members of rival Tamil groups and hostages held for ransom.

LTTE forces have committed numerous gross abuses of human rights including the massacre of hundreds of non-combatant Muslim and Sinhalese men and women in attacks on their communities and in attacks on buses and trains. They have tortured and killed prisoners, and abducted people for ransom. They have also executed prisoners whom they accused of being traitors.

Women have been murdered, raped, taken hostage and tormented by armed opposition forces in many parts of the world. Many of these groups claim to be fighting for the rights of those they abuse.

Both women and men have been murdered and mutilated by the armed opposition in Mozambique — the Mozambique National Resistance (RENAMO) — particularly during the mid- to late 1980s. Some women captured by RENAMO were forced to carry heavy loads of looted goods back to RENAMO bases, some were forced to become "wives" of RENAMO officials.

In Sudan the two factions of the rebel Sudan People's Liberation Army (SPLA) hold large parts of the south of the country. Fighting between the SPLA factions has displaced tens of thousands of southern Sudanese civilians: women, men and children, many of them helpless victims of famine, have been maimed and killed despite taking no part in the disputes.

In Angola the armed opposition UNITA, which refused to accept the results of UN-sponsored elections in 1992, has continued its campaign of terror. When UNITA forces gain control over areas where there is strong support for the government, young men of military age and community leaders are often killed and women raped. In May 1993 UNITA troops in Huila province ambushed a

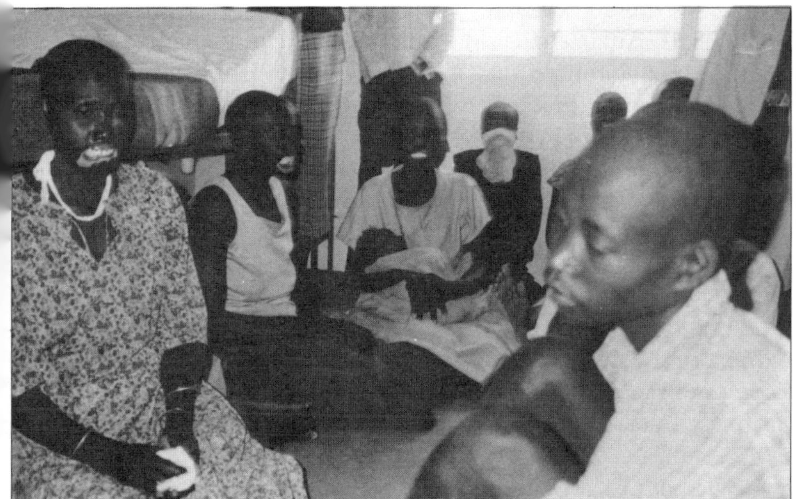

These women from Awere, Kitgum district, Uganda, had their mouths and noses cut off by members of the United Democratic Christian Party (UDCA) in 1991. Mutilation was widely used by UDCA rebels to punish civilians suspected of cooperating with the authorities. Armed opposition groups all over the world have resorted to brutal abuses of women. © Nathan Etengu

train and then bayoneted some of the survivors, including women and children.

Several armed opposition groups in the Americas persistently use torture and murder to further their political aims. Women living in rural areas of Peru find themselves "caught between two fires"; they are targeted both by government soldiers and by Shining Path. Accurate information about the total number of people killed in the conflict is not available. However, credible sources put the number of victims at more than 27,000 and suggest that half were killed by Shining Path and half by the government's security forces. A significant proportion of both government and opposition killings did not take place in armed combat; they were murders.

Shining Path has killed election candidates, mayors and other local and regional officials. Its victims also include members of non-governmental human rights organizations; journalists; priests, nuns and others attached to the Roman Catholic and evangelical churches; political activists from across the political spectrum; and leaders of popular organizations not in sympathy with Shining Path's aims and methods. In addition, the organization has summarily killed thousands of peasants they accused of collaborating with government forces or who had refused to support Shining Path. On 18 August 1993 Shining Path hacked to death at least 62 men, women and children in the province of Satipo, Junín department. Three days later, Herminia Barboza Oré, a community leader in the neighbourhood of Cruz de Mopute, San Juan de Lurigancho, Lima, was shot dead in her home by Shining Path.

In Colombia, guerrilla organizations such as the Revolutionary Armed Forces of Colombia (FARC) and the National Liberation Army (ELN) have carried out numerous attacks in which defenceless women and men have been killed. Scores of people have been kidnapped and held to ransom; some have been killed in captivity. Others, including journalists and local government officials, have been taken hostage by guerrilla forces and sometimes held for prolonged periods before being released, often under obligation to carry messages to the government about proposed negotiations.

Asia has also seen long-running conflicts in which women have paid the ultimate price for other people's ambitions. Women's lives have been devastated by opposition abuses in countries such as Bangladesh, Pakistan, Papua New Guinea and the Philippines.

In India, armed Sikh groups fighting for independence in the state of Punjab have abducted, raped and ill-treated women. Some women have been forced to marry members of these groups. Majir Kaur was kidnapped in Tarn Taran in June 1992 by members of the Khalistan Liberation Army (KLA). She was raped and forced to marry a member of the Khalistan Commando Force, which is loosely affiliated to the KLA. Rape by armed militant groups has also been reported from the Indian state of Jammu and Kashmir, gripped by civil war for the past four years. In February 1993 a 19-year-old woman from Handwara told journalists in Delhi that she had been raped by members of one of the militant groups.

In Algeria, killings of women by militant Islamic groups have coincided with drastic clampdowns by the government and a sharp deterioration in respect for human rights.

A state of emergency was imposed in Algeria in February 1992 after the cancellation of multi-party elections following the success of the opposition Islamic Salvation Front (FIS). Since then, more than 10,000 people have been killed by the security forces, Islamist groups and other armed groups. Scores of women have been killed in Algeria since the beginning of 1993 in attacks attributed to armed Islamist groups.

Women throughout Algeria have faced increasing pressure

from armed Islamist groups to wear the Islamic veil and to stop travelling on public transport because male and female passengers are not segregated. A young woman was killed as she got off a bus in April 1994 in Ben Zergia, an Islamist stronghold to the east of Algiers, apparently because she had broken the prohibition on women using public transport. Katia Bengana, a 16-year-old student, was shot dead in Mefta (Blida) in February 1994 reportedly after receiving threats that she would be killed if she did not wear the *hidjab* (Islamic veil). After her death the Organization of Young Free Algerians (OJAL) put out a statement saying that for every woman killed for not wearing the veil, they would kill 20 veiled women and 20 "bearded fundamentalists". Soon after

Barzani women in Qoshtapa, Iraq. They are holding photographs of their husbands, some of the 8,000 Kurds of the Barzani clan who "disappeared" at the hands of the Iraqi forces in August 1983. In a speech President Saddam Hussain said that "those people were severely punished and went to Hell ...". The authorities have never acknowledged these arrests. Most families of the "disappeared" in Iraq are still waiting for news of their relatives. © Brenda Prince/FORMAT

that, on 29 March 1994, two young women students wearing the veil were shot dead at a bus stop near their school.

In Israel the Islamic Resistance Movement (*Hamas*) has continued to target Israeli civilians during the peace process. A suicide car bomber killed four women, two girls and a man in April 1994. The attack was described by *Hamas* as "legitimate retaliation" for the murder of at least 29 Palestinians by an Israeli settler in Hebron in February 1994.

Large parts of the northern Iraqi provinces of Duhok, Arbil, Sulaimaniya and Kirkuk have been controlled by Kurdish opposition groups since October 1991. Human rights abuses have been widespread in this area, which is formally administered by the Council of Ministers for Iraqi Kurdistan. Among the political prisoners held in Iraqi Kurdistan were four women: Laila 'Ali Musa, from Hakkari, Turkey; Tibat 'Abdallah Sulaiman, from Bahdinan; Payman Sulaiman Hamid, born near Shaqlawa, Iraq; and Dalal Hezel Adina, born in Diyarbakir, Turkey. They were arrested in August 1992 in Arbil during a demonstration held to protest against the Turkish military bombardment of Sirnak in southeastern Turkey. The demonstrators were violently dispersed by the Kurdish security forces who killed two and injured several others. Two members of the security forces were also killed.

One of the dead was the six-year-old daughter of Laila 'Ali Musa. Interviewed in prison in December 1992, she gave Amnesty International the following account:

> *"When the shooting started I was immediately hit. Then my daughter Kurdistan was killed as a bullet shot through her head. Tibat ['Abdallah Sulaiman, a co-detainee] was also injured with three bullets ... After the shooting they arrested a group of us and took us inside the Asayish building. They tortured me for about one and a half hours in one of the offices. They beat me on the bullet wound and on my back with a hosepipe. They took the injured ones, myself and Tibat, as well as my dead daughter, to the Emergency Hospital. We stayed there two days and then they took the two of us to* al-Mahatta *Prison."*

Until the 1990s Amnesty International did not address abuses by armed political groups, although it condemned the torture or killing of prisoners by anyone, including these groups. In 1991 Amnesty International decided to actively oppose other deliberate and arbitrary killings and hostage-taking by armed political groups, a policy change which has meant increased action to protect individuals from abuses by these groups.

No political group — regardless of the provocation — has the right to deprive those who take no part in the conflict of their lives or liberty. The basic standards of international humanitarian law are the absolute minimum requirement; under no circumstances should they be breached.

Victims of the 'New World Order'

The end of the Cold War raised hopes for greater freedom and democracy around the world. Many believed the "proxy wars" sponsored by the two superpowers of the previous era would be speedily resolved and that the world would become a more peaceful place. But this promise of a new world order did not meet the expectations it had raised.

The former Soviet Union

For women living in the former Soviet Union, the disintegration of the previous system has led to great upheavals. Violent conflicts have erupted throughout the region as borders are contested and claims by particular ethnic or national groups are pursued, sometimes with violence.

Many women have been forced to flee from their homes, seeking safety elsewhere, within or beyond their own country. The journey itself is a source of danger and abuse. Those that remain at home must struggle with the shortages and price increases for essential goods, the dislocation of services and the daily burdens of living in a war economy.

For some women, the impact is even greater. They are the ones caught up in the conflict: as combatants, as the wives, mothers, sisters and friends of combatants, or just because of where they live.

In the remote former Soviet republic of Tadzhikistan, Yevanigina Davlatshoyeva, a student in her early 20s, stood in a bread queue on a street in the capital, Dushanbe. It was December 1992. She was seized by a group of armed men and shot dead on the spot. Yevanigina Davlatshoyeva was apparently killed because she came from the Pamir mountains in the far east of the country, a region believed by government supporters to be a centre of opposition. Her murderers are believed to have been members of the People's Front of Tadzhikistan, a paramilitary body which carried out "law-enforcement duties" for the government.

Since factional violence erupted in Tadzhikistan in May 1992, armed conflict between forces divided along both political and regional lines has left up to 20,000 people dead, according to official estimates, and displaced more than 600,000 people. Women and children have figured prominently among the displaced, and have been tortured and murdered by all sides.

In Azerbaijan whole families have been taken hostage in the bitter armed conflict over the Nagorno-Karabakh region, which is mainly populated by ethnic Armenians. Both the Azeri authorities and ethnic Armenian paramilitary forces have taken hostages with the apparent intention of exchanging them for prisoners held by the other side.

Six Azeris, three women and three children from the same family, were detained by ethnic Armenian forces in February 1992 as they tried to escape from fighting around Khodzaly, a town in Karabakh. In August 1993 a released Azeri hostage reported seeing two of the women being forced to work on a cattle farm in the Shusha district. The town of Shusha had fallen to ethnic Armenian forces in May 1992, giving them overall control of the disputed enclave.

The aftermath of the Gulf conflict

Samira Ma'arafi, a 27-year-old woman who ran her own small import/export business and loved to paint, was arrested by Iraqi soldiers in November 1990. She was seized at a check-point in Kuwait City during the Iraqi occupation of Kuwait. Since then there has been a wall of silence about her from the Iraqi authorities. Her mother, who has campaigned tirelessly for her release, has had to rely on fragments of news: that her daughter was in jail in Kuwait; that she had been moved to Iraq. The last reported sighting of Samira Ma'arafi was in 1992, when a Lebanese man said he had seen her on a prison bus in Baghdad.

The Gulf conflict of 1990 and 1991 is receding into history, but in Kuwait and Iraq its aftermath continues to dominate women's lives. Some are grieving over the loss of loved ones. As well as the military casualties, hundreds of unarmed civilians were murdered in Kuwait by Iraqi troops. Victims included children shot in the head at close range whose bodies were then dumped outside their homes.

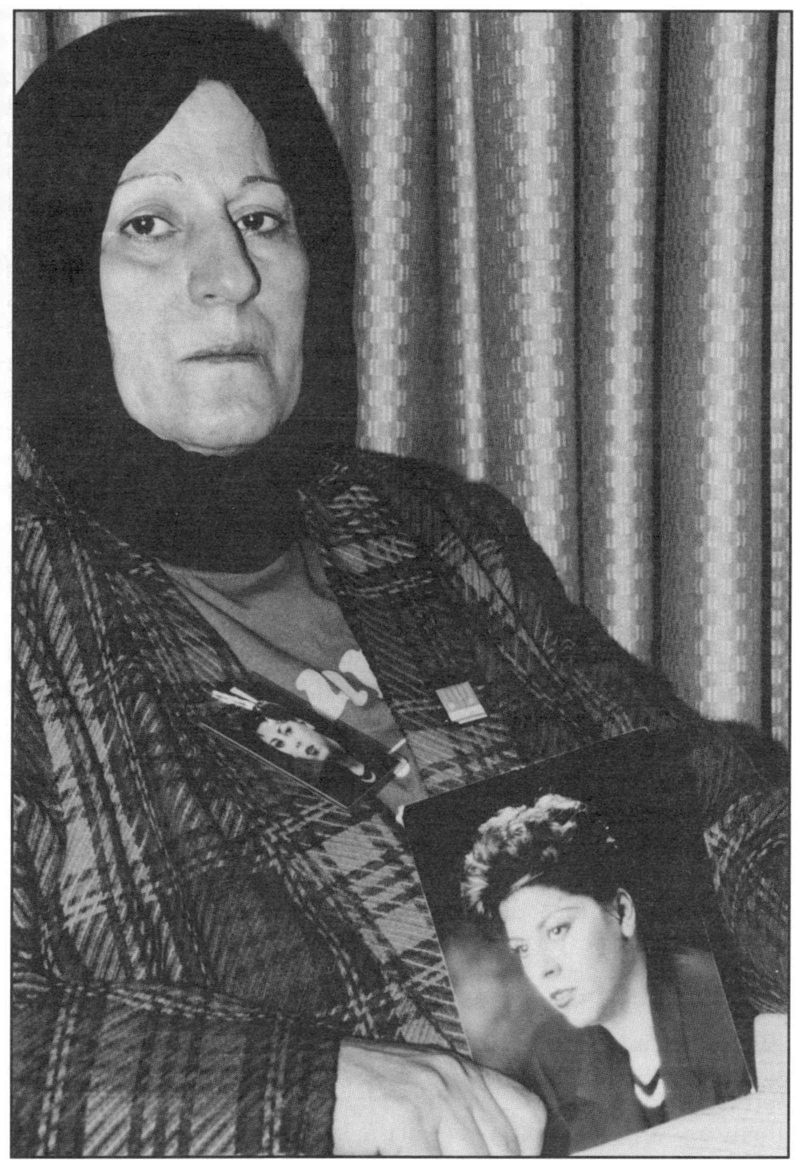

Baheeja Ma'arafi holds a photograph of her daughter, Samira, who was arrested in Kuwait by Iraqi soldiers in November 1990. The last reported sighting of Samira Ma'arafi was in 1992 in Baghdad. © Ferhat Azizi/ **New Statesman & Society**

Although allied forces succeeded in expelling Iraqi troops from Kuwait in February 1991, they did not intervene when Iraqi Government forces crushed mass uprisings by Kurds in the north of the country and Shi'a Muslim Arabs in the south in March 1991. Thousands of people went into hiding in the vast southern marshlands area which has traditionally served as a hiding place for government opponents and army deserters.

Since then, there have been repeated government attacks on the marshes. The government has drained large stretches of marshland, destroying the local economy, and has deliberately attacked villagers, both men and women. Several hundred people were killed or injured on 26 September 1993 during military attacks on villages in the southern marshes. A UN team which visited the area in November announced subsequently that it could not confirm or deny allegations that chemical weapons had been used.

When the Iraqi Government released thousands of prisoners of war and civilian detainees in 1991, it claimed that all prisoners arrested in the course of the conflict had been released and sent back to Kuwait. At least 625 people — among them Samira Ma'arafi — simply "disappeared".

In addition, UN-imposed sanctions against Iraq have had a disastrous effect on the Iraqi economy, affecting all but the most rich and powerful. Women, trying to feed and care for themselves and their children, are hit hardest.

In Kuwait itself, following the withdrawal of Iraqi troops in February 1991, scores of people were murdered by Kuwaiti forces and armed civilians in a wave of revenge killings. Victims included Palestinians, Iraqis and Sudanese living in Kuwait who were singled out because of their nationality and shot in public or tortured to death in secret. Hundreds of people were arbitrarily detained and at least 62 "disappeared" in custody.

Since then, the Kuwaitis have mounted a series of manifestly unfair trials. In 1991 and 1992 more than 120 people — many of them prisoners of conscience — were sentenced to long prison terms for "collaborating" with the Iraqi occupation forces. Among them are 15 former employees of the Iraqi-run newspaper *al-Nida'*. Their entire trial lasted just one day. Defendants were not allowed to cross-examine the key witness against them, a "secret source" who never entered the courtroom.

Six defendants, including Ibtisam Berto Sulaiman al-Dakhil, a 35-year-old woman journalist and a prisoner of conscience, were sentenced to death, later commuted to life imprisonment. Others were sentenced to long prison terms. Wafa' Wasfi Ahmad, a 23-year-old Jordanian secretary, said that she was forced to work for *al-Nida'* by Iraqi soldiers. She is a prisoner of conscience, serving a 10-year sentence in Kuwait Central Prison.

What price peace?

For more than 20 years, 900 Greek Cypriot women have been waiting to see their husbands, unsure whether they are alive or dead. The men "disappeared" when Turkey invaded Cyprus, an invasion which led to the division of the island along ethnic lines. When prisoners of war were exchanged in September 1974, Elli Stavrou went with her children to the Red Cross point to greet her husband. "We went every day until November, when all the prisoners were returned. Then we realized he wouldn't be coming home."[8]

The wives of men missing since the 1974 Turkish invasion of Cyprus protest at their continued "disappearance". © Pam Isherwood/FORMAT

For the 900 wives, the uncertainty has lasted half a lifetime. Only 20 have remarried. By law, they could apply for a divorce after seven years but powerful social forces made this difficult or impossible for most. In 1975 more than 200 Turkish Cypriots were also missing; their families still have no information about their fate and, to Amnesty International's knowledge, the Greek Government has yet to provide any.

The end of armed hostilities does not mean the end of the story for the women whose lives have been irrevocably disrupted by conflict. Some have lost loved ones — husbands, sons, brothers and sisters — for whom they will grieve for the rest of their days. Some have to care for those physically or psychologically disabled by war and conflict, who will never again be able to lead independent lives. Some have to come to terms with their own traumatic experience of conflict — assault, rape or even mutilation. Some have been forced to abandon their homes and their roots.

The most pressing aspect of conflict resolution for most people is to find out what has happened to their husbands, their wives, their children and their friends.

> *"This is why I demand justice, to some day know if my wife was murdered, which is most probably what they did to Mónica; but they should have the courage to say where her body is so that we can give her a decent burial like any human being, and an exemplary punishment to those who planned or carried out thousands of killings, so that this never again happens in our country."*
>
> Manuel Maturana Palma, Santiago, 1986

For years after Mónica Chislayne Llanca Iturra "disappeared", her husband, Manuel Maturana Palma, campaigned to find out what happened to her and to the hundreds of others who "disappeared" while Chile was under military rule. The National Commission for Truth and Reconciliation (CNVR), set up shortly after the civilian government took office in March 1990, established that at least 957 people "disappeared" following their abduction by the security forces. Preliminary investigations carried out by the National Corporation for Reparation and Reconciliation, which replaced the CNVR in 1992, have established that at least 1,097 people "disappeared".

Mónica Llanca Iturra was taken from her home in the early hours of 6 September 1974 by members of the Directorate of

National Intelligence (DINA), which was disbanded in 1978; the DINA was responsible for most of the "disappearances" and other gross human rights violations committed between 1974 and 1977. Although a witness saw Mónica in 1975 in a detention centre used by the DINA to hold detainees after they had been tortured, the Chilean authorities consistently denied all knowledge of her arrest or whereabouts. To this day her family do not know what became of her.

An amnesty law passed in 1978, which granted immunity to the perpetrators of human rights violations, has been used by the courts to block full investigations into cases of human rights violations. Charges against a senior DINA agent arrested in connection with the "disappearance" of Mónica Llanca Iturra were revoked in July 1994 under this law.

There can be no lasting peace without justice. Justice requires that the truth be established. The victims and society have a right and a duty to know what has happened to the "disappeared" and who was responsible for abuses of human rights. Justice requires that the guilty be held accountable for their actions. If those who have committed human rights violations in the past do so with impunity, the ground is laid for further abuses in the future.

Justice requires compensation for the victims. There can be no adequate compensation for a woman who has lost her husband, or her health and hopes, or years of her life. But inadequate though they are, reparations must be made to those who have suffered human rights violations.

Thousands of women and teenage girls from Korea, China, the Philippines, Indonesia and other nations, were forced into prostitution by the Japanese military before and during the Second World War. The Japanese Government has denied for decades that the military authorities were involved in schemes to procure so-called "comfort women" (*ianfu*) for soldiers and officers of the Japanese army in Asia. However, the government has recently admitted the military's involvement and political leaders have issued formal apologies for the atrocities committed. But claims for compensation to victims have consistently been denied and no official has been brought to justice in connection with what amounted to the use of sexual slaves by the military.

Historians estimate that 100,000 to 200,000 women were forced into prostitution as military "comfort women". The women were transported by the Japanese military to front-line areas in China and

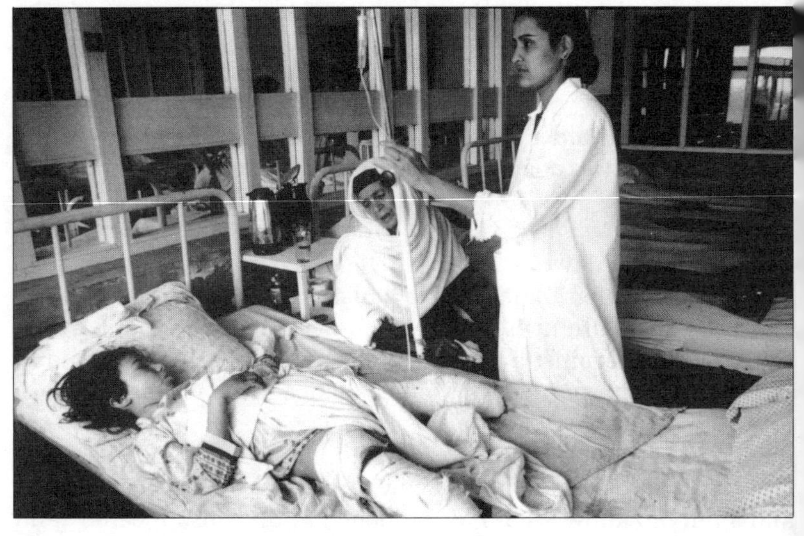

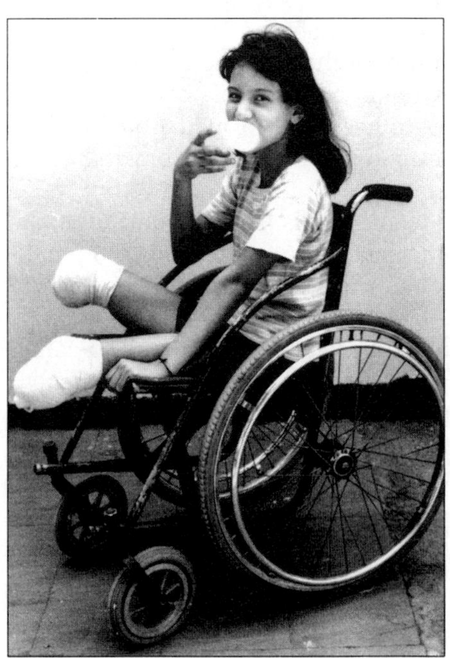

"Mines are fighters that never miss, strike blindly, do not carry weapons openly and go on fighting long after hostilities are ended ... the greatest violators of international humanitarian law, practising blind terrorism."
Red Cross spokesperson

In virtually every modern conflict thousands of people are killed and injured by landmines laid by government and armed opposition forces alike. The landmines are often deliberately placed in rural areas to kill or maim civilians who have taken no part in the conflict.

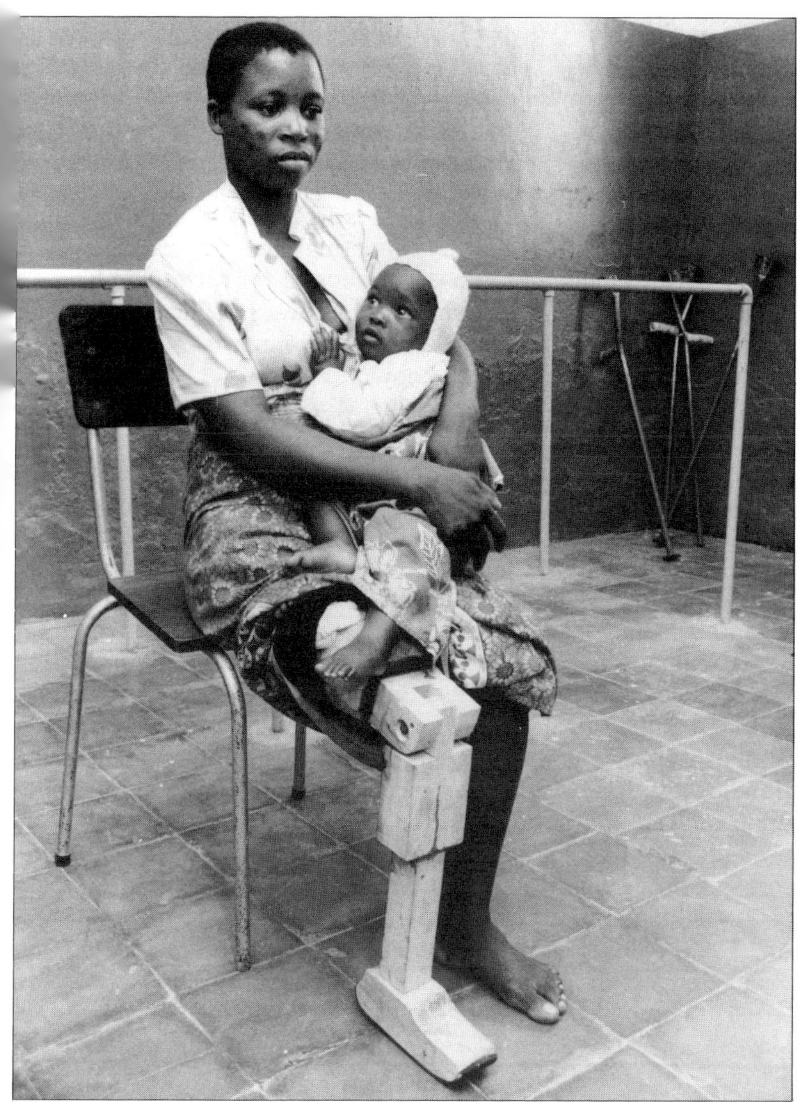

Above: *A landmine victim is fitted with an artificial leg at a Red Cross centre in Mozambique. © Jenny Matthews.* **Left top**: *A 12-year-old Afghan girl, who lost both her legs when she stepped on a landmine near her village, waits in Kabul hospital for an operation. © Howard J Davies.* **Left bottom**: *Kenya, a young landmine victim in Managua, Nicaragua's capital city © Jenny Matthews*

across South-East Asia. Former "comfort women" have testified that they were forced to have sex with dozens of soldiers every day, in "comfort stations" controlled directly or indirectly by the military.

Many of the "comfort women" reportedly died as a result of untreated sexually transmitted disease, harsh punishment or indiscriminate acts of torture. Others were left to die near front-lines at the end of the war by retreating Japanese armies. While Asian governments and non-governmental organizations have in recent years published the names of hundreds of surviving former "comfort women", the total number of women who suffered this ordeal will probably never be known.

In August 1993 the then Prime Minister Hosokawa Morihiro expressed "condolences" to women and other victims of the "aggressive and wrong" war waged by Japan. These same sentiments were expressed in August 1994 by Murayama Tomiichi, the then Prime Minister, when unveiling a plan to spend one billion US$ over five years on projects related to the Second World War. However, the government has refused compensation to former "comfort women".

The Japanese Government's position is that all compensation claims were settled in the 1951 San Francisco Peace Treaty and in other treaties between Japan and individual Asian nations. A number of non-governmental organizations, including the International Commission of Jurists, have encouraged the authorities to grant such compensation, and some former "comfort women" have brought civil damages suits against the Japanese Government before Japanese courts. None of these have so far resulted in compensation being granted.

The UN Sub-Commission on Prevention of Discrimination and Protection of Minorities decided in August 1993 to appoint an expert to study and prepare a report on "systematic rape, sexual slavery ... during wartime". However, funding for this research was withheld under a March 1994 decision of the Commission on Human Rights. In August 1994 the Sub-Commission recommended a study into the issue of the impunity of those involved in organizing the "comfort women" scheme in Japan. To Amnesty International's knowledge, no Japanese official has ever been brought to justice in connection with human rights violations related to the forcible use of "comfort women".

2

Women activists

Norma Corona Sapién paid with her life for trying to protect the human rights of others. She was gunned down in a "death-squad"-style killing in Mexico on 21 May 1990, almost certainly because of her work as a human rights lawyer.

She was President of the independent Commission for the Defence of Human Rights in Sinaloa state. At the time of her murder she was investigating the case of a Mexican lawyer and three Venezuelan university professors who were reportedly abducted by federal judicial police agents. The bodies of the four men, all showing signs of torture, had been found near Culiacán, the state capital of Sinaloa, in February 1990. Norma Corona immediately started investigating the killings. Soon after, she began receiving death threats which she believed came from federal police agents.

Her killing triggered a wave of national and international criticism of the Mexican Government's human rights record. The government promised that "things would change", and shortly afterwards created the National Human Rights Commission whose first major task was to investigate the murder of Norma Corona. In September 1992 a federal judicial police commander was arrested and charged with the murder and is currently awaiting trial. However, several others allegedly involved with the killing have not been brought to justice.

Norma Corona is a symbol of the millions of other women around the world whose names are not widely known but who have stood up for their principles, regardless of the personal cost. The cases of some of these women are described below. Not one has encouraged or participated in violence. Every single one has been the victim of some form of violence.

Most were not targeted because they were women — they were singled out because their activities were perceived as a threat by the authorities. In some cases, however, because they were women they were subjected to particularly vile forms of harassment, torture or ill-treatment.

They all have one thing in common. They are women who wanted to improve their societies and decided to do something about it. They are political opponents of the government, imprisoned for advocating social change. They are trade unionists killed for organizing workers. They are human rights activists who are victims of the violations they are trying to stop. They are lawyers who are targeted for daring to defend the poor. They are community activists who are persecuted because they are seen as a threat to the established order. They are mothers, sisters, wives and daughters who are victimized simply because they protest about the "disappearance" of a relative.

Women at a rally held in Algiers in 1992 in defence of democracy and women's rights © Janina Struk/FORMAT

These are, or were, courageous and determined activists. That is why they were targeted.

Trade unionists

All over the world women are forced by economic necessity into miserable factories with miserable rates of pay. Employers demand women workers whom they see as cheaper and more docile than men. Sometimes, however, the appalling conditions encourage women to organize and fight back. But when they take up the struggle for their rights they are seen as a threat by those in power. This can mean that they lose their jobs. It can also cost their lives.

Marsinah's body was found by a group of children in a shack at the edge of a rice field some 100 kilometres from her home. It was bloodied and covered in bruises. There were strangulation marks on her neck. A blunt instrument had been thrust into her vagina causing terrible injuries.

A few days earlier she had been a lively 25-year-old leading a strike at the watch factory where she worked in Porong, Sidoarjo, East Java, in Indonesia. She was brutally murdered, almost certainly by the military, because she was a trade unionist who stood up for workers' rights.

In Indonesia factory workers suffer terrible exploitation. Even according to the government-run trade union, the official rate of pay is less than a third of that considered necessary for physical survival. Women workers fare even worse — taking home on average half the male wage. In 1992 the independent Legal Aid Institute (LBH) published a report showing that women also have worse hours and conditions, often suffer various forms of abuse and maltreatment, and are invariably fired if they become pregnant.

In the watch factory where Marsinah worked, the management decided it would not even pay the official minimum wage. So on 3 May 1993 the workers walked out.

The military authorities, including the Commanders of the District Military Command (KODIM) and the Sub-District Military Command (KORAMIL), quickly responded to this act of defiance by interrogating workers about their role in the strike. Meanwhile, the strikers became organized. Marsinah was elected as one of 24 worker representatives who immediately opened negotiations with the company. The following day they announced that almost all of their demands had been met.

Yeni Damayanti outside the Central Jakarta District Court, Indonesia, in March 1994. She and 20 other students were sentenced to six months' imprisonment in May 1994 for "insulting" President Suharto. The sentences were later increased, following an appeal by the prosecution, to between eight and 14 months. The students had been arrested in December 1993 for demonstrating against human rights violations under the government of President Suharto.

Before they could celebrate, however, the representatives learned that 13 workers had been summoned to the local KODIM headquarters. Marsinah spent the evening compiling a series of written guidelines for her colleagues to use when responding to interrogation.

The next morning, 5 May, the military told the 13 workers that they had to resign or face charges for holding "illegal meetings" and "inciting" others to strike. During the interrogations, some of the workers were beaten and one was threatened with death. Marsinah drafted a protest statement to the company. After giving the statement to a colleague, she went to the military headquarters to look for her colleagues. Later that evening she met some friends. She left them at 9.20pm, saying she was going home to eat. Three days later her body was found.

Pressure from labour activists and human rights groups forced the police to open an investigation, but it was quickly taken over by military intelligence authorities. In November 1993 nine of the watch factory's staff and executives, and one military officer, the KORAMIL commander, were charged in connection with the murder and brought to trial. However, the procedures used suggest that the real purpose of the prosecutions was to obscure military responsibility for the killing. Several of the accused were detained by military intelligence officers, held incommunicado for up to three weeks and forced to confess to the murder, some of them under torture. During the trial, all nine civilian defendants retracted their statements given under interrogation. By July 1994 all the civilians had been found guilty: seven were sentenced to between 12 and 17 years in prison, one to four years and one to seven months. The KORAMIL commander was charged only with a disciplinary offence for failing to report a crime to his superiors. He was sentenced to nine months in jail and was not discharged from the army.

A thorough investigation by the LBH concluded that high-ranking military authorities were responsible for Marsinah's murder. Even the National Human Rights Commission suggested that "other parties" might have been involved. In late November 1994 the High Court in East Java overturned one of the guilty verdicts, adding fuel to demands for a new investigation and for those sentenced to be released. There is little chance, however, that those responsible for killing Marsinah will be brought to justice.

When governments allow their security forces to kill and intimidate trade unionists with impunity, the cycle of violence can go on for generation after generation. The tragic story of Sara Cristina Chan Chan Medina and her family powerfully illustrates the consequences. The story also shows that many women are not cowed by the terror. Instead, they often become the bravest defenders of workers' rights.

In 1980, 10-year-old Sara Cristina watched her father being shot dead by Salvadorian soldiers because he was a prominent trade unionist. Nine years later, on 19 August 1989, she "disappeared" — reportedly abducted by air force personnel because she worked for the trade union federation FENASTRAS. Her mother, María Juana

Antonia Medina, who also became involved with FENASTRAS, has suffered a series of gross violations of her human rights.

Witnessing the fatal consequences of being an active trade unionist might have scared off many people. But for Sara Cristina, the memory of what happened to her father was not something she could ignore. When she was 18 she decided to report on the plight of the trade union movement through the lens of a camera, becoming a photographer for FENASTRAS.

The authorities did not ignore her family. A year later, in July 1989, her mother was detained in Santa Ana and taken to the headquarters of the Second Infantry Brigade, where she was tortured. A few days later she was released without charge.

A month later, María Juana learned of her daughter's "disappearance". She searched everywhere. She ignored repeated threats and continued to visit military bases, police centres and government offices, demanding to know where her daughter was. She presented a writ of *habeas corpus* before the Supreme Court asking for her daughter's detention to be clarified. The Court failed to process the complaint.

Like her daughter, María Juana chose not to hide from the terror. Instead, she committed herself to helping FENASTRAS while continuing the search for Sara Cristina.

On 18 September 1989 she joined a demonstration organized by FENASTRAS in San Salvador to protest against recent arrests of trade unionists. She was arrested and taken to the National Police headquarters. There she was blindfolded and beaten with rifle butts. Then she was raped. She was released without charge only after "confessing" to having joined the Farabundo Martí National Liberation Front (FMLN) to avenge the death of her husband and the "disappearance" of her daughter.

A month later a bomb went off in the FENASTRAS offices killing 10 people, including a witness to Sara Cristina's abduction. Among the injured was Sara Cristina's younger sister.

The armed conflict between the government and the FMLN ended in January 1992, with the armed opposition group becoming a legal political party. A Truth Commission was established, which raised hope that those responsible for human rights abuses during the conflict would be made to pay for their crimes. The family of Sara Christina had reason to hope: her case was one of 32 the Commission chose to investigate in depth.

In March 1993 the Commission published its report. It confirmed what the authorities had so vigorously denied — that Sara Cristina "disappeared" in the custody of the air force. Despite this, justice was not done. Just days later, the government passed a sweeping amnesty law which shields from prosecution the perpetrators of killings, torture, rape and "disappearances" during the armed conflict. Such action means that nothing has been done to stop the violations continuing for yet another generation.

Adela Agudelo is another young woman who probably paid with her life for her commitment to trade unionism. She worked with FENSUAGRO, a peasant trade union in Colombia, and was involved with an agricultural cooperative. She "disappeared" in April 1992. She was 24 years old.

On the morning of 5 April she took a bus for Paipa to visit the thermal baths for medicinal reasons. A few minutes later two armed men in civilian clothes boarded the bus. They announced they had come for "the guerrilla whore" and forced Adela Agudelo off the bus. The driver and passengers say they saw her being driven to the army's Sylva Plaza Battalion headquarters near Tunja, Boyacá department.

The battalion denied all knowledge of her arrest. The Presidential Adviser on Human Rights said an investigation was under way, but this was apparently inconclusive. In late May or early June 1992, Adela Agudelo was seen by someone she knew in Duitama square in the company of soldiers. She dropped a piece of paper on which she had scribbled that she was being held in the First Army Brigade at Tunja. The Procurator General's Office ordered an inspection of the First Brigade and the Sylva Plaza and Bolívar Battalions, but she was not found. However, there was a bizarre incident during the inspection. The Commander of the First Brigade saw a member of the Judicial Police with a woman, who looked remarkably like Adela. He said, "What, you found her?" In fact, the woman was the police officer's secretary. The judge asked the General if he knew Adela: "How do you know that she resembles the person we are looking for?"

The killers of Margarida Alves made no mistake about her identity. They went to her home in August 1983 and shot her dead because she was President of the rural workers' trade union in Alagoa Grande, Paraíba state, Brazil. She had received many death threats from landowners and sugar mill employers. At the time she was killed she was involved in negotiations over pay and conditions for sugar workers.

Between 1983 and 1987 no less than five public prosecutors were assigned to and then transferred from the investigation into her murder. A trade union lawyer, Teresa Braga, who took up the case, received death threats and her home was bombed. In 1987 the authorities from neighbouring Pernambuco state asked for the records of the case as they had uncovered evidence that both Margarida Alves and a trade union lawyer had been killed by a "death squad" of military and civil police operating in the region. Since then, however, no progress appears to have been made towards bringing her killers to trial.

Women trade unionists are also at risk in Guatemala. Elizabeth Recinos Alvarez de León, a member of the National Assembly of Public Health Workers and a leader of the Union of San Vicente Hospital, and Eluvia de Salam, a leader of the Social Welfare Union and member of the National Federation of Guatemalan Trade Unionists were both abducted in Guatemala City by unidentified men in June 1993. Eluvia de Salam was released the next day. Elizabeth Recinos was drugged, beaten and kicked. Two of her ribs were broken. She was found unconscious outside Eluvia de Salam's house a week later. As far as Amnesty International is aware, no investigation into the incident has been set up.

Political activists

Dr Ma Thida is sitting in a cell. There is barely any light. She is alone, as she has been for more than a year. She is 27. If the Burmese state has its way, she will not see open spaces again until she is 46.

Dr Ma Thida is one of at least 75 women who are being detained in Myanmar as prisoners of conscience or political prisoners. At the time of her arrest in mid-1993, she worked at the Muslim Free Hospital in Rangoon. She was also a well-known fiction writer. Like her friend, Aung San Suu Kyi, for whom she was a campaign assistant in 1988 and 1989, Dr Ma Thida is being punished solely for her political views and peaceful activities.

There are many other women around the world who are behind bars just because they want to see greater democracy in their countries. For this reason Maria Elena Aparicio Rodríguez spent more than two years in prison in Cuba. She joined the Harmony Movement (MAR), a human rights organization which works for democratic socialism, and became the group's coordinator for

Havana, the Cuban capital. MAR published a clandestine newsletter called "Solidarity and Democracy". She worked at the National Conservation and Museums Centre and she was arrested when she was caught reproducing the newsletter there.

In early 1992 the government decided it was time to hit back at MAR. It declared, without any apparent evidence, that MAR was forming secret cells to carry out violent attacks. It seemed it was particularly irritated that Maria Elena and the MAR leader were trying to recruit members from within the government and the army. On 2 February 1992 Maria Elena was arrested, accused of urging civil unrest, sabotage and attacks on security forces, and charged with "rebellion". No evidence was ever presented to support these charges.

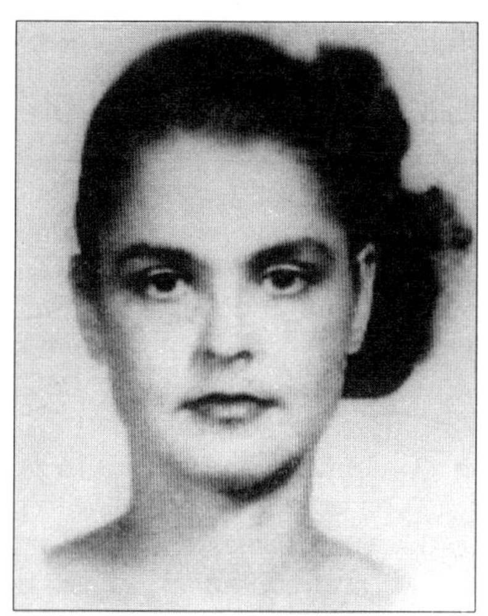

Maria Elena Aparicio Rodríguez, a human rights and pro-democracy activist, spent more than two years in a Cuban prison.

Her trial appears to have been grossly unfair. She was given limited access to a lawyer and was not allowed to speak in her own defence. She was convicted and sentenced to seven years in prison. In January 1993 she joined other political prisoners in the women's prison in Havana in a protest against a reduction of prison visits. She was then moved to Guanajal Women's Prison, far from family and friends. In October 1994 she was released on condition she left Cuba. She is now in Spain.

On the other side of the world, Zhou Ying and Zhou Yongfang were jailed for wanting political reform in their country. They are just two of the thousands of pro-democracy activists who were detained in China after the 1989 protests were brutally crushed. The two young women, the first a student at Nanjing Chinese Medical College, the second an office worker, were both arrested in late 1990 in Jiangsu province by the Public Security Bureau. They were accused of involvement with "a counter-revolutionary clique", the China Democratic Frontline, and were reported to have been tried on 1 April 1991 in Jiangsu province.

Chen Minlin has been in prison in China for even longer. She was one of many women who pushed for reforms in the build-up to the 1989 protests. As a teacher she organized meetings at her school and took part in pro-democracy demonstrations. In the climate of terror which prevailed after the protests were crushed, she was denounced by some of her students. She was arrested on 15 June 1989 in Guangzhou, Guangdong province, and sentenced to eight years in prison.

The Chinese authorities responded with even more brutality when Ngawang Kyizom made a protest — a protest which lasted just 90 seconds. That was how long it took her to shout "Long Live the Dalai Lama" and "Free Tibet" at the entrance of a Buddhist shrine in the Tibetan capital Lhasa. For this outburst in September 1990, Chinese secret police kicked and beat her, jabbed her with an electric cattle prod on her tongue, breasts and thighs, and then jailed her for three years without a proper trial.

Women make up nearly a third of the hundreds of political prisoners held in Tibet. Many have been tortured. Most are nuns serving sentences of two or three years of "re-education through labour".

Rigzin Choenyi, also a nun, will be in captivity for much longer than this. She has been a prisoner of conscience since 1989 and will not be released until 2001. Her crime? She too shouted slogans.

Rigzin Choenyi's story is not unusual in Tibet. In September 1989 she and five other nuns shouted pro-independence slogans in a market in central Lhasa. The authorities accused them of breaking "martial law regulations". Rigzin Choenyi was sentenced in October 1989 to seven years' imprisonment.

Prison did not dampen her spirit. In March 1992, for instance, she and about 25 other women inmates at Drapchi Prison in Lhasa demanded to wear their civilian clothes to mark the Tibetan New Year. The prison authorities refused, but the women went ahead anyway. They also voiced their commitment to Tibetan independence. The authorities called in the People's Armed Police, a militia administered by the army, who reportedly beat the women. All sustained injuries on their arms and legs; some were injured on their bodies. Rigzin Choenyi was then put in solitary confinement for at least a month.

In a similar case, a nun serving a nine-year sentence, imposed in 1989, had her sentence extended by eight years in October 1993. This was Phuntsog Nyidron's punishment for collaborating with 13 other nuns to record pro-independence songs on tape recorders that had been smuggled into the prison. On the tape each of the 14 nuns announced their names and dedicated a song or poem to their friends and supporters. On one tape are the words: "Our food is like pig food, we are beaten and treated brutally. But this will never change the Tibetan people's perseverance: it will remain unfaltering."

Many women in Iran are also serving long prison sentences for peacefully opposing the government. Shaheen Sameie has been behind bars since her arrest in 1982. She is serving a 15-year sentence for alleged support of the left-wing organization *Peykar*. Shaheen Sameie, a factory worker in her forties, was tried in secret in Evin Prison in 1983. She was also allegedly tortured and denied access to legal counsel. She cannot appeal against her conviction or sentence.

Vasiliya Inayatova is a poet and human rights activist. She is also a member of *Birlik*, Unity, an opposition movement in Uzbekistan, which advocates a secular democratic system. In 1993 these three aspects of her life landed her in court. She was charged with "infringement upon the honour and dignity of the President", a serious offence under the Criminal Code. What the authorities found offensive was her poem, "Last letter to the President", published in September 1992, in which she wrote about an unnamed leader who used guns against students. In February 1993 Tashkent City Court sentenced her to two years in a corrective labour colony. She was spared this ordeal under the terms of an August 1992 presidential amnesty, which led to her immediate release.

Just over a year later, however, she was arrested again, this time for trying to attend a human rights conference in Almaty,

Kazakhstan. On 12 May 1994 Uzbek police reportedly detained her after she had crossed the border into Kazakhstan. They took her and several companions back to Tashkent where they were interrogated at the police headquarters for five hours. Her friends were released, but Vasiliya Inayatova was charged with "insulting a police officer". She was held as a prisoner of conscience under "administrative arrest" for a week.

Elsewhere, women political activists are intimidated by different means. On 19 May 1994 the offices of the Salvadorian Women's Movement (MSM) in San Salvador, El Salvador's capital city, were broken into and ransacked. Important documents were damaged. The following day Alexander Rodas Abarca, a reserve member of the National Civilian Police, was killed as he was guarding the MSM offices.

No one knows who organized these attacks, but they appear to be part of a campaign of intimidation by elements linked to the Salvadorian military and civilian authorities. Police investigations into the incidents have been opened, but no results have been announced.

Many women around the world have been targeted for championing social reform. In some cases, they have been victims of the very crimes they have been struggling to eradicate.

Mirentchu Vivanco Figueroa, for example, a member of the "Sebastián Acevedo" Movement against Torture in Chile. She was detained on 29 March 1992 by *Carabineros* in Villa Francia, Santiago. She says she was taken to the 21st Police Station where she was beaten on the legs, nearly asphyxiated, and had her hair violently pulled. The next morning she was taken to the 38th Police Station, where she alleges she was deprived of sleep and made to walk blindfold for hours in the interrogation room. She was also denied access to her lawyers. She was released in February 1993.

Mamura Usmanova wants better conditions for women in Uzbekistan. She is a leading member of *Tumaris*, an unofficial organization which campaigns for women's and human rights. For this reason, apparently, she and her family were attacked and threatened. On 7 December 1993, the day she was due to travel to Bishkek, capital of neighbouring Kyrgyzstan, to attend a human rights conference, unknown assailants broke into her home. The men held a knife to her throat and told her to "keep your mouth shut" or else there would be more trouble. Her daughter was also assaulted, as was her husband who suffered concussion, a fractured rib and internal bruising. The attackers searched the apartment and took away papers and personal documents. They left the valuables.

Activists promoting women's issues in India have also been victims of brutal treatment. In February 1994, for instance, the Progressive Organisation of Women (POW) collaborated with two other non-violent organizations to hold a convention in the town of Karimnagar, in the southern state of Andhra Pradesh, on "Democratic Movements and the Constitutional Machinery". When the district authorities banned the event, the POW organized a silent march through the town. The women walked in pairs in accordance with police regulations in force in the area.

Suddenly the police attacked the silent protest. They beat women with *lathis* and rifle butts, particularly on the breasts and

Women protest against the continuing violence in Colombia. Since 1986 more than 20,000 people have been killed in Colombia for political reasons; most were killed by the armed forces and their paramilitary protégés. Many women human rights activists have been among the victims. © Jenny Matthews

Professor Wangari Maathai, a founder of the Green Belt Movement, was detained, ill-treated and hospitalized twice within the space of a few weeks in early 1992 by members of the Kenyan security forces.

between the legs. They threw women on the ground and trampled on them. They tore off their blouses and saris, and abused them with foul language. Many of the women were then thrown into a lorry and taken to prison. The next day they appeared before a magistrate, who remanded them in custody and refused to record their statements alleging molestation and assault by the police. The women were then taken to the Warangal central prison where they were strip-searched and subjected to other abuses. An inquiry into the incident concluded by defending the police action.

Professor Wangari Maathai, an internationally renowned environmentalist and a founder of the Green Belt Movement in Kenya, was detained, ill-treated and hospitalized twice within the space of a few weeks in early 1992.

On 13 January 1992 she was arrested at her home in the capital, Nairobi. Her house had been surrounded by police since 10 January, when she and others had claimed at a press conference that they had evidence proving that the government intended to hand over power to the army. She was released on bail on 14 January having been charged under the Penal Code with "publishing a false rumour which is likely to cause fear and alarm in the public". Almost immediately she had to go into hospital as her chronic rheumatism had been exacerbated by being forced to sleep on the police cell's concrete floor without a mat or blankets. The charge was later dropped.

Professor Maathai was not deterred by this experience. Two months later she joined a protest known as the "Mothers' Hunger Strike" outside All Saints Cathedral in Nairobi — a peaceful campaign for the release of political prisoners. On 3 March riot police attacked the vigil and she and three other women hunger-strikers were beaten unconscious. All four needed hospital treatment. As soon as Professor Maathai had recovered, she vowed to continue the campaign by the Release Political Prisoners group.

Two women political activists in Ethiopia were detained in January 1994. They were held in Godey in eastern Ethiopia after demonstrations against the central government and during mass arrests of members or suspected members of the Ogaden National Liberation Front (ONLF). In January the ONLF won the majority of seats in the regional assembly and was campaigning for a referendum on self-determination and independence for Ogaden. The central government opposes its demands. Hajio Dama, the 65-year-old chairwoman of the Ogadenian Women's Democratic Alliance (OWDA), was released after some weeks, seriously ill. Korad Ahmed Salal, also an OWDA official, died in custody in unexplained circumstances. A third OWDA official, Ibado Abdullahi (known as "Gabya", meaning "poet") was detained in Degabur on 20 March: at the time of writing there were fears for her safety.

Women are among the many hundreds of political activists who have been frequently arrested in Sudan. Sara Nugdallah, a university lecturer and member of the executive and women's committees of the banned Umma Party, has been repeatedly detained for her political activities. The last time she was arrested was on 7 April 1994. She was initially held in the security headquarters before being transferred to Omdurman Women's Prison. She was released on 20 June. No reason was given for her arrest. She had been arrested several times before, most recently in March 1994 when she was held for a few hours before being released uncharged.

Governments that punish women for their political activities often end up punishing children as well. Among the many infant victims is Kamilya, the daughter of Doha 'Ashur al-'Askari, who has never known anything but prison life. She was born in Duma

Women's Prison in the Syrian capital Damascus in July or August 1993, a few months after her mother was arrested for suspected membership of the Party for Communist Action (PCA). Doha 'Ashur al-'Askari had been living in hiding since 1986, when the authorities said they wanted to arrest her in connection with the PCA. In the same prison, for the same reason, are Fadwa Mahmud, Khadija Dib, Tuhama Ma'ruf, Silya Abbas and Raghda Hassan. Fadwa Mahmud has been separated from her two children since March 1992. At the time of writing, all six women were being tried by the Supreme State Security Court.

Human rights activists

In countries where government forces can kill and maim their opponents with impunity, it is especially important that local people stand up for human rights. Without them, human tragedies go unrecorded and the forces of terror can carry on without fear of exposure — let alone punishment. It is in precisely these situations that those who do stand up for human rights are particularly vulnerable.

In many such countries, women have thrown themselves into the fight for human rights. They speak out, often putting themselves and their families at risk, perhaps realizing that if they don't, no family, including their own, will ever be safe.

The three children of Blanca Cecilia Valero de Durán had such a mother. She was the secretary of the Magdalena Medio Human Rights Regional Committee (CREDHOS), in Colombia. For several years the organization has monitored and denounced human rights violations by the Colombian armed forces and paramilitary groups, as well as condemning abuses by armed opposition groups in the region. It also offers support to the victims and their relatives.

Located in one of the worst areas in Colombia for human rights violations, all those who join CREDHOS know only too well the risks they face. Staff members continually receive threats, and the threats are sometimes carried out.

Blanca Valero continued her work despite the intimidation. At 6.30pm on 29 January 1992 she left the CREDHOS office. Two men in civilian clothes were waiting for her. They fired several times at her at point-blank range. She died almost instantly. According to witnesses, three policemen watched the attack without attempting

Three of the "Mothers of Acari" hold a press report about the "disappearance" of 11 people in Magé, Rio de Janeiro State, Brazil. In their efforts to have the "disappearances" properly investigated the mothers have faced a concerted campaign of intimidation. In January 1993 one of the mothers was killed shortly after she had testified in court about police involvement in the "disappearances". © Américo Vermeltto/Istoé

to intervene. They did not even try to catch the assassins, who escaped and have never been caught.

In early January 1994 a Colombian daily newspaper reported that two naval officials had testified to the Attorney General about their assignment in 1991 to a secret Navy Intelligence Unit, identified as Network 7, which operated under the direct command of the national director of Naval Intelligence. The officials described how the unit had assassinated about a hundred trade unionists, teachers, journalists and human rights workers — including Blanca Valero — in the city of Barrancabermeja and throughout the Magdalena Medio region. However, judicial investigations into the unit's activities have reportedly been passed to the military justice system, which has consistently failed to convict members of the armed forces involved in human rights violations.

The security forces in the Philippines thought a dose of intimidation would be enough to scare Maria Socorro "Soki" Ballesteros into giving up her work as a human rights educator for Amnesty International-Philippines. Six men who described themselves as policemen abducted her and her husband, Niel, in Quezon City on 11 October 1993. They took them blindfold to a secret "safehouse" and interrogated and threatened them. Soki was questioned about her human rights work and Niel was forced to agree to become a military informant. A few hours later, when the abductors believed they had achieved their objectives, the couple were freed.

Far from being frightened into silence, Soki and Niel immediately called a press conference where they described their ordeal and denounced the authorities. Soki said: "Being a human rights educator, I believe in the UN principle that human rights are first and foremost a state responsibility. In our case, where the perpetrators were members of the military, the Philippine Government should be held accountable." She added that she and her husband would prosecute those involved in their abduction as she believed doing "something about it" would help minimize such violations in the future. Their home is kept under surveillance and they continue to be warned that they are being tracked by the military.

Another human rights activist in the Philippines has also experienced first-hand the intimidatory tactics of the security forces. In early 1994 Sonia Soto, 33, began campaigning on behalf of two peasant activists who were killed by armed men alleged to be members of the 172nd unit of the Philippine National Police (PNP). Since then she has been repeatedly threatened by men in plain clothes believed to be linked to the PNP. On 26 February, for example, she was stopped by several men who told her: "How are you Ms Soto? We've just been to your house. We know you. Be careful. You will be next." She too has vowed to continue her work.

Ayse Nur Zarakolu is a Turkish human rights activist and publisher who has been repeatedly persecuted by the authorities. She is married with two children, and has been involved in various political, publishing and trade union activities. She is also a member of the Istanbul branch of the Human Rights Association.

As director of Belge Publishing House, she was sentenced on 1 July 1993 to five months' imprisonment for publishing in June 1991 a book about Turkey's Kurdish minority by Ismail Besikçi. Her sentence was confirmed by the Court of Appeal and on 4 May 1994 she was arrested and began serving her sentence in Sagmalcilar Prison in Istanbul. She was released at the end of August. She faces further prosecutions for publishing other books by the same author.

Ayse Nur Zarakolu was no stranger to persecution. In 1982 she had been remanded in custody for three months for publishing documents from the Turkish Communist Party's founding congress. In late 1984 she had been remanded for a further six weeks for employing people alleged to be members of illegal political parties.

One method of intimidation used against people in Honduras who press for human rights abuses to be investigated is the issuing of death threats. On 2 March 1994, for instance, Berta Oliva de Nativí, the General Coordinator of COFADEH, a committee of relatives of the "disappeared", was making a telephone call when the line was intercepted by a man who identified himself as a colonel. He threatened to make Berta Oliva "disappear" and to kill her and her family. The telephone threats were repeated several times that day and again 12 days later. Some calls played a funeral march.

Community activists

Women the world over are involved in community activities. They organize support networks. They set up health and education projects. They run crèches. These activities allow women to make greater contributions to their societies and in most places are seen as a valuable addition to community life. In some places, however,

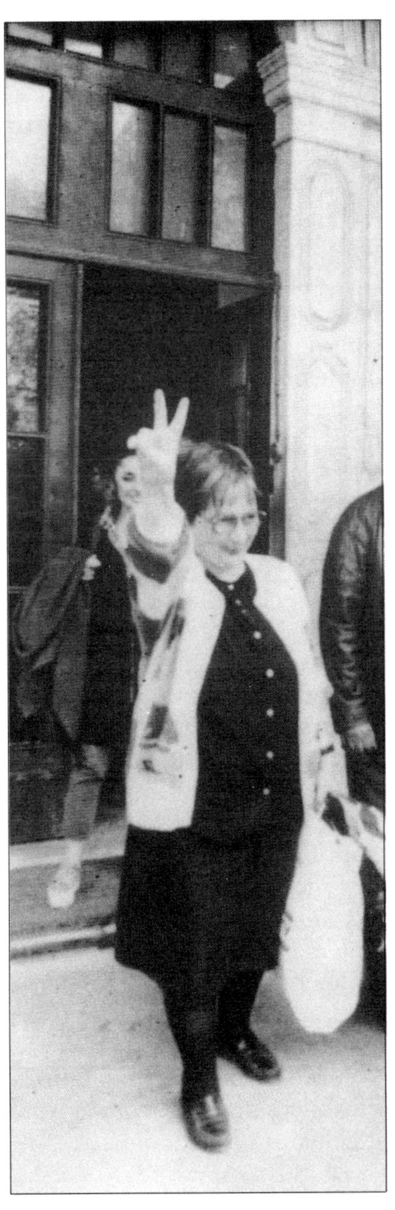

Ayse Nur Zarakolu, a Turkish human rights activist and publisher, has been repeatedly persecuted by the authorities.

governments view these community activities as a threat. They are not directly controlled by them and persist in standing up for basic human rights. So they are targeted. The women involved may be falsely accused of supporting opposition groups. The groups may be banned. Sometimes their members are terrorized or even eliminated.

In Peru the authorities often accuse people of sympathizing with Shining Path, and then deal with them accordingly. Such was the fate of Santosa Layme Bejar, whose only "crime" appears to have been helping women's and children's health projects in her community. In 1983 she became involved in local projects in her home district of San Juan de Lurigancho, in the capital Lima. She helped set up the *Vaso de Leche* (Glass of Milk) program, which feeds the needy. Since 1989 she has been the area coordinator for her neighbourhood. In February 1994 she was detained by members of DINCOTE, the anti-terrorism branch of the police, in her home district. She was accused of being a Shining Path member and charged with "crimes of terrorism".

The charge arose because she was accused by a Shining Path member of being involved in *Nueva Red*, New Network, a Shining Path support network. In fact, just before her detention she received a letter from Shining Path which threatened her with death if she did not provide them with food from the *Vaso de Leche* program. She has consistently made public her unqualified opposition to the activities of the armed opposition in Peru. In 1991, for example, she joined a march for peace in response to the killing of two community leaders by Shining Path.

There is absolutely no evidence to suggest that Santosa Layme has links with Shining Path. She has neither used nor encouraged violence. She is a prisoner of conscience, held by a government which has used wide-ranging anti-terrorism laws to imprison hundreds of people who face charges which appear to be politically motivated.

Hundreds of abandoned and orphaned children live desperate existences on the streets of Guatemala's cities. They are sometimes attacked by "death squads", beaten and persecuted by the police, and survive on the edge of starvation. Their only hope and comfort comes from women and organizations who dedicate themselves to easing their plight. For this work, the "street educators" are themselves singled out by the security forces for abduction, torture, rape, intimidation and threats. They often have to deal with the bloody consequences of attacks on street children by the security forces, and are therefore seen as a potential threat as witnesses.

Olga Odilia Jiménez Fajardo, a nurse, worked temporarily as a social worker with an organization helping street children. One day in March 1990, when she was working in San Juan de Dios Hospital, she recognized a street child, Nahamán Carmona, who had been wounded by a police officer. The boy told her about the attack, and although she made sure he received proper treatment, he died. She also took photographs of the boy in hospital, proving that he had been there and had been able to speak before he died.

A few months later her nightmare began. In November 1990 three men driving a black car without licence plates stopped her as she was walking home. They told her she had a lot to tell them and warned her against having foreigners in her home (a US lawyer and an Australian journalist had reportedly been renting rooms in her house). In March 1991, again as she was walking home, two men in a car warned her that she would be abducted and sexually abused. They said they were sparing her this time because she had her young daughter with her. Two months later, on 15 May, a man in plain clothes tried to abduct her as she was going to work. She escaped by hitting him in the stomach.

Just 12 days later, however, she was abducted. Four men, believed to be members of the security forces, forced her into a car. Half an hour later she was told to get out of the car and get undressed. They asked about the foreigners living in her house, about her work and about whom she had spoken to about Nahamán Carmona. One of the men then raped her. She was later released and required hospital treatment. On 29 August 1991 two other men again tried to abduct her, but she escaped. She subsequently fled the country.

Crusaders for justice

Rosa Pu Gómez' husband "disappeared" in Guatemala in 1981, two days after her first child was born. When the baby was two months old, Rosa's father "disappeared". Nine years later Rosa's second husband "disappeared".

This series of personal tragedies turned Rosa into an activist. She did everything she could to find her missing relatives. She also became involved with the National Coordinating Committee of

Widows of Guatemala (CONAVIGUA), and is now a leading member of the committee.

As a result she has faced a campaign of terror. She has been followed by unknown men and has received many death threats. In January 1992 she was seized at gunpoint by a man who interrogated her about leaders of grassroots organizations. Later she was named on lists of "targets" issued by "death squads" linked to the security forces. One, published in October 1993, named 20 people, including Rosa, who would be considered military targets if they did not leave the country within 72 hours. She refused to flee and remains in Guatemala at great risk.

When governments allow their forces to abduct, kill or secretly imprison political opponents, they hope their acts of violence and the victims will be quickly forgotten. They have not reckoned on the determination and courage of the victims' relatives — often the wives or mothers whose lives have been shattered by the state's arbitrary use of its powers. These women frequently transform their lives overnight to become crusaders for justice. They will not let the authorities get away with their crimes unchallenged.

Dr Manorani Saravanamuttu is a symbol for the mothers, wives and companions of the tens of thousands of people who have "disappeared" or been murdered by government forces in Sri Lanka. A medical doctor and daughter of one of the island's wealthy élite, her life was suddenly propelled into a world of death, grief and intimidation when her son, Richard de Zoysa, a journalist, was abducted and killed in Colombo in February 1990.

Three months after the murder, a letter arrived at Dr Manorani Saravanamuttu's house with the regular post. It warned: "Mourn the death of your son. As a mother you must do so. Any other steps will result in your death at the most unexpected time ... Only silence will protect you. Heed this advice. Your son failed to heed advices [sic] and had to be killed ..." It was signed: "Justice Honour and Glory to the Motherland".

She refused to be silent. She campaigned vigorously to expose the truth about her son's killing and for the murderers to be brought to justice. She told whoever would listen that she could identify one of her son's abductors as a Senior Superintendent of Police in Colombo. She also has good reasons for believing the other abductors were police officers stationed in Colombo. Despite her determination, no independent inquiry into her son's abduction and killing has been held, and the police inquiry has produced no results.

She also defiantly ignored the repeated threats against her by taking on a leading role in the Mothers' Front, a mass movement of 25,000 mothers of Sri Lanka's "disappeared". She is now working in a rehabilitation and counselling centre for victims of violence in Colombo.

"They expect you to curl up in a corner and die of fear," she told the *Washington Post* newspaper in 1991. "The women are saying 'We are going mad with grief at home alone.' Now at least we are doing something."

Edméia da Silva Euzébio was another mother who refused to remain silent about the "disappearance" and probable murder of her child. Her son, Luiz Henrique da Silva, was one of 11 youths abducted in July 1990 from a farm in Magé, in the Brazilian city

Dr Manorani Saravanamuttu whose son, Richard de Zoysa, was abducted and killed in Sri Lanka. "They expect you to curl up in a corner and die of fear ... The women are saying 'We are going mad with grief at home alone.' Now at least we are doing something." © Brigitte Voykowitsch

Rio de Janeiro, allegedly with the involvement of civil and military police. None of the youths was ever seen again.

She too ignored repeated death threats and campaigned vigorously for an investigation to find the youths. In January 1993 she paid for her bravery with her life. She was walking in downtown Rio de Janeiro with her friend, Sheila da Conceição, when two men approached in broad daylight, called out her name and shot both women dead. A few days earlier Edméia had testified about police involvement in the "disappearances".

In Honduras a woman working with COFADEH played back the messages on the group's answering machine in June 1994. She jumped away from the male voice in horror. "Listen bitches, stop searching for your puppies because they are dead. Be careful what you do, stop talking to the radio and television. You do not want more disappeared, do you? Otherwise you will be the next ones."

The caller identified himself as *Sanidad Social* (Social Sanitation), a "death squad" active in Honduras in the 1980s. The threat

Relatives of soldiers at a demonstration in front of a Yugoslav army base in Croatia in August 1991. They were calling for the men to be demobilized from the Yugoslav army.* © *Filip Horvat/SABA-REA

was one of many made against COFADEH. It is widely believed that the threats may be connected with the intelligence service of the Honduran Armed Forces, disgruntled at recent steps taken to clarify what happened to the "disappeared" and to hold the perpetrators to account.

Zhang Fengying has never committed a crime. She is not a political activist. She doesn't belong to any group. She simply wants medical care and justice for her husband, Ren Wanding, who is serving a seven-year prison sentence for making speeches during the pro-democracy movement in China in 1989. For this she has faced persistent persecution.

In 1991 Zhang Fengying and her daughter were evicted from their home in the capital, Beijing. Their belongings remain sealed in the apartment to this day. After their eviction they drifted from one temporary home to another, being constantly harassed by the police. The authorities have pressed her to leave the capital, but she refuses. In July 1993, the police detained her and her daughter for six days. They were not charged.

Many wives of Chinese dissidents have suffered similar fates for refusing to accept quietly the wrongful jailing or killing of their husbands. They face not just harassment and repression from the authorities, but also the daily worry about their spouses' health in prison and how to keep the family going.

Lawyers

Meral Danis Bestas discovered that the law in Turkey offered her no protection when, as a lawyer, she tried to defend human rights. She has acted in many political cases and has represented clients making official complaints against the Turkish security forces for torture and other human rights violations. She was secretary of the Diyarbakir branch of the Human Rights Association (HRA) in November 1993 when she was detained incommunicado for four weeks in Diyarbakir Gendarmerie headquarters. She told Amnesty International:

> *"For three days I was interrogated several times about my work for the Human Rights Association. During this time I was slapped, kicked and insulted, including crude sexual insults which I found very upsetting. They asked why the HRA did not defend soldiers. I answered that our position*

towards the PKK *and the army was clear, that we stood up for civilians and those not involved in the conflict ...*

"Eventually on 9 December they prepared a statement of four pages and asked me to sign it while still being blindfolded. I said 'I'm a lawyer, I am not going to sign anything I have not seen.' They threatened to torture me. I replied that torture was a crime against humanity and they should not do it. They took off my clothes and soaked me for an hour with freezing water. I was terribly cold ... I was kicked and beaten ..."

Diyarbakir State Security Court released her but her trial for allegedly supporting the PKK continues.The real reason for her persecution appears to be her work for human rights.

In Brazil women lawyers who have been brave enough to stand up for the rights of the poor have become victims themselves. Márcia Maria Eugênio de Carvalho, for instance, frequently defended rural workers in labour suits against powerful local landowners. In January 1993 she was killed by unknown gunmen who ambushed her car near Recife, the state capital of Pernambuco.

At the time of her death she was working on a number of court cases on behalf of rural workers. Reportedly, Márcia Maria Eugênio de Carvalho had been advised by fellow lawyers to take extreme care owing to the fear of reprisals from landowners whose interests she may have been affecting. On the day of her assassination Márcia Maria Eugênio de Carvalho was returning to Caruaru from the town of Barra de Guabiraba where she had met several rural workers. To Amnesty International's knowledge, nobody has been charged with her killing.

In Colombia lawyers who conduct independent inquiries or act for the defence in political cases are at risk. Lourdes Castro García, who acted for left-wing guerrilla leader Francisco Galán, has been repeatedly threatened by the military police holding her client. They have accused her of an association beyond the professional, saying things like "If you are Galán's lawyer, then you must share the same ideology". Too many Colombian human rights lawyers have been killed or have "disappeared" to ignore such warnings. As is the case with most political killings and "disappearances" in Colombia, little effort has been made to find those responsible.

Victims of their conscience

Many women around the world have paid a heavy price for standing up for their principles. Some expected to suffer. Others, however, believed that their right to act according to their conscience was protected in their country's constitution.

Dr Yolanda Huet-Vaughn is a US physician. She was also an army reserve captain. When the US Government announced in 1990 that it was taking military action against Iraq after the invasion of Kuwait by Iraqi forces that August, she thought that as a physician, a reservist and a citizen she had the right to protest. She opposed the offensive against Iraq because she feared heavy civilian and military casualties, and huge environmental damage. She also believed the international blockade was working.

She was ordered to report to Missouri's Fort Leonard Wood. There she was told of a new military procedure for applications to become a conscientious objector — review of such claims could not interrupt service at the front. She left the base on 30 December 1990 and did not return. That act triggered her court martial. She gave herself up on 2 February 1991 and on 6 March that year was charged with desertion. Her request for conscientious objector status had been filed on 21 February and the army chaplain agreed then that she was a conscientious objector. On 9 August 1991 she was found guilty of "desertion with intent to shirk hazardous or important duty" and sentenced to 30 months' imprisonment. The sentence was later reduced to 15 months, and she was released after serving eight. For those eight months she was a prisoner of conscience.

3

Women at risk

Left: ***A Tzutuhil woman in Santiago Atitlán, Guatemala. Indigenous communities bore the brunt of the army's counter-insurgency operations in the 1970s and early 1980s. Many of these communities were virtually destroyed.***

At risk in custody

"They snatched me off the street. I put up a fight against the security police, but they hit me on the head with a pistol butt and I passed out. Images swarmed in my head. My mother's and father's faces haunted me. One method used by Iraqi jails epitomizes their barbarity. And that is rape ... No matter how much I'd heard about it, nothing prepared me for the actual experience. It lives on inside me. I still bleed a lot. It was done not by just one man, but by a group of them. They stifled my screams and protests. I had to give in. And it was a side-show; lots of people came to watch."

Kurdish woman, member of the Iraqi Communist Party *Pesh Merga*, in the late 1980s

No country in the world treats its women as well as men. Women from all social classes, cultures and races, in all societies, are at risk of abuse of their human rights. Discrimination in civil society can compound the risk to women's human rights. Often, discrimination against women is reflected in national law. If the law regards a woman as a second-class citizen, where is the incentive or the opportunity for society as a whole to respect women's human rights?

Certain groups of women are particularly vulnerable to human rights violation. Women taken into custody in many countries are at risk of rape and other sexual torture and ill-treatment. In several countries judicial systems discriminate against women by sentencing them more harshly than men convicted of the same offences. Some judicial systems provide cruel, inhuman and degrading punishments for crimes for which most offenders are women. Women who come from minority or marginalized groups are in

Nebile Tabak (right) *was 18 years old when Turkish soldiers raided her village on 12 July 1994. They were looking for weapons, but reportedly found none. They seized Nebile, her father and three other girls and paraded them in front of the other villagers, insulting them and hitting them. Then they took them away to the Gendarmerie headquarters in Igdir. They were held incommunicado, and reportedly tortured before being released on or around 18 July.*

double jeopardy. Discriminated against as women, they are also the victims of prejudice.

Dawa Langzom, a nun, was arrested in 1989 in Lhasa, the Tibetan capital, after shouting pro-independence slogans during a demonstration. In the police jeep on the way to Gutsa detention centre, the arresting officers cut off one of her nipples with a pair of scissors, according to nuns who have now fled Tibet.

Another Tibetan woman, 26-year-old Sonam Dolkar, was arrested in July 1990 because she was suspected of pro-independence activities. Although she denied any political connections, she was interrogated under torture every other day for six months. She endured a fearsome range of torture techniques. She was stripped naked, slapped and punched. She was wrapped in electric wires and given electric shocks until she fainted. She was prodded all over her body and on the face with electric batons. Electric batons were pushed into her vagina. She was restrained in handcuffs and leg-irons throughout her ordeal and held in solitary confinement on the days she was not tortured. After a while, her memory started to deteriorate and she became increasingly weak and sick. She often vomited and urinated blood after being tortured with electric current. During interrogation, she would often collapse and her interrogators would beat her to make her stand up. By early 1991 she was vomiting and urinating blood every day and was in such condition that a doctor was finally called to see her. The doctor said she would die if she was given more electric shocks and the torture then stopped. She was eventually transferred to a police hospital from where she managed to escape. She left the country clandestinely during the second half of 1991.

Rape is a form of torture experienced by women all over the world. Rape and threats of rape are often used to elicit information or a confession during interrogation. Rape and sexual abuse are also used to humiliate and intimidate women and thus weaken their resistance to interrogation, or to punish them.

Sometimes women are raped solely because police officers and soldiers think they have the right to do so. One of two young factory workers raped in East Java, Indonesia, in January 1993 said the soldier who raped her had boasted: "Go ahead and report us to the commander. He's not going to do a thing. This is our right!"

Women were singled out for rape and sexual abuse when the military launched an anti-poaching operation in Zaire's Salonga National Park during April and May 1992. Over a dozen schoolgirls aged between 13 and 15 were detained and raped by soldiers and gendarmes forced a man to rape his 18-year-old daughter at gunpoint in front of other detainees. Ilanga Nsongi, alleged to be a poacher's wife, was arrested and tortured. She was two months pregnant and miscarried as a result of the torture. She was then raped. Mutu Impala Sidonie was among a group of women arrested and then repeatedly raped in front of their husbands. To Amnesty International's knowledge no action has been taken against those responsible.

In many countries the social stigma attached to rape and sexual abuse amounts to a rapists' charter of impunity. Rape by the security forces is a particularly oppressive form of torture as many women are too afraid and ashamed to speak out about their experience. These were the feelings of a 23-year-old woman arrested in Bhutan with her husband in 1990 and detained in an army camp in Sarbhang district. Interviewed by Amnesty International in a refugee camp in Nepal, she said that soldiers had raped her two or three times a night for three months.

> *"On release I went home where I stayed for one month until I realized I was pregnant. I was so ashamed that I couldn't face the other villagers so I left Bhutan in early January 1991. I left my children with my mother-in-law. I went into the jungle, hoping I would die there ... As a result of the rape, I had twins, one of which died ... I do not know if I will see my husband again."*

In January 1993 an assistant sub-inspector in the Delhi police force allegedly raped a young married woman, after detaining her on the pretext that she was of "a dubious character". In March 1993, the Supreme Court ordered the police chief of Haryana state to personally investigate charges that a 13-year-old girl had been raped by two men and subsequently tortured in Samalkha police

Indian women take to the streets of the capital, New Delhi, to protest against rape and sexual abuse. © Associated Press

station. In 1993 an 11-year-old girl was gang-raped by police officers in north-east Delhi. In November 1993 a young woman was gang-raped by police officers searching for her husband. Her husband committed suicide two days later. In April 1994 a 22-year-old woman charged police officers in north Delhi with having raped her.

Hundreds of cases of police rape have been reported in India in recent years, but convictions of police officers for raping women in their custody remain rare. Few cases of custodial rape reach the trial stage. In 1990 five police officers in West Bengal were suspended for allegedly repeatedly raping Kankuli Santra in Singur police station. The police at first tried to avoid responsibility by claiming Kankuli Santra was mentally ill. They then said she was a "bad" woman. Public protests eventually forced charges to be brought against two of the officers, but the case was dismissed for "lack of evidence".

An average of 30 women are raped in India every day, according to official statistics. Only a small fraction of these rapes are committed by police officers. However, when law-enforcement officials are seen to be able to rape women without fear of prosecution, this clearly signals to society at large that the authorities do not treat the crime seriously.

India is far from being the only country where this occurs. Rape and sexual abuse by state agents are rarely treated seriously by governments. In most cases, investigations are not carried out and those responsible, if they are punished at all, suffer only minor disciplinary sanctions.

In Chile Tania María Cordeiro Vaz, a Brazilian, was arrested with her 12-year-old daughter in March 1993 and taken to Santiago. During the first week of her 18 days in incommunicado detention she was reportedly raped, tortured with electric shocks, beaten and kicked. Her daughter, who was held for five days, was threatened with her mother's death. Tania Cordeiro presented a formal complaint to the courts, but those allegedly responsible were not taken into custody and although several police officers were charged with illegally arresting her, none was charged with torture or rape.

Riccy Mabel Martínez, a 16-year-old student, was raped and murdered by soldiers in Ocotal, Honduras, in July 1991. In 1993 an army colonel and a sergeant were sentenced to 16 and 10 years' imprisonment respectively after being convicted of raping and killing her. Her family lodged an appeal against the sentence, arguing that the officers should have been convicted of murder rather than the lesser crime of manslaughter, for which they were given minimum sentences. A test case of the military's accountability before the law, the trial was obstructed by threats against the judge and the prosecutor, and attempts by the military to have the accused tried before a military court, which were countered by intense pressure from fellow students and human rights campaigners.

The US state authorities did take action when, in September 1992, a scandal erupted over widespread sexual abuse in a Georgia women's prison. But for several years previously they had failed to investigate properly reports of abuse at the Women's Correctional Institution, a women's prison at Hardwick.

The scandal came to light when 70 women prisoners filed affidavits over a period of four months alleging that prison guards were responsible for rape, sexual abuse, prostitution, coerced abortions, sex for favours, and retaliation for refusal to participate. For several months the authorities played down the allegations. Eventually 14 prison officials were charged, several were dismissed and senior state officials resigned. "There had been for years rumours of sexual abuse, forced abortions, and a prostitution ring being operated out of the state prison for women, but we could never prove it," Robert W. Cullen of Georgia Legal Services told the press. "Now, we finally have the evidence and it is much worse a problem that we ever suspected."[9]

According to the senior official brought in after the scandal erupted in 1992, "We reacted way too slowly to the [earlier] allegations ... Our staff was not properly trained to handle female offenders. The regular reporting method of inmate complaints did not work when it came to sexual harassment. There was no attention at all to women's services".[10]

Forced gynaecological examinations

"I was arrested on 31 December with four friends from outside the newspaper office ...We were taken to Çankaya police station, Ankara. We were blindfolded in the car, and our hands bound behind our backs. On the way up the stairs our heads were banged against the walls. They started to remove my clothes, which I tried to obstruct them from doing. Then they started to squeeze my breasts. They threw us to the ground and jumped on top of us ...

"They handcuffed our hands behind our back, making comments all the time and poking and pawing us ... [When] I struggled against their handling, they said: 'Do you enjoy that? So you like a bit of roughness,' and other sexual remarks. Two of them came over to us, and touched our hips and legs. Another policeman tried to force his foot into my mouth. One of them urinated on me. We were generally sexually molested. They wanted to know if I was pregnant, how many people had I slept with. They said they would give me a virginity test."

Ferda Mazmunolu, journalist on *Alinteri* (Toil) magazine, 1994.

In recent years Turkish police have increasingly used virginity tests as a means of degrading and humiliating women.

The use of virginity testing in Turkey as a means of criminalizing, threatening and abusing women was recently documented in a report from Human Rights Watch (HRW).[11]

Two groups of women are particularly vulnerable to forced virginity testing: women suspected of prostitution, and women detained for political reasons. In June 1992 the head of the Security Department in Adana told the press that female political detainees, "militant girls", were being subjected to virginity examinations to avoid future accusations of police abuse during interrogations.[12] An attorney in Diyarbakir, capital city of southeastern Turkey, provided HRW with documentation on several cases in which women detained as members of the Kurdish armed opposition group PKK were taken for forced virginity tests by state forensic medical doctors. In October 1993 *Özgür Gündem* reported that a translator working for a German delegation on a fact-finding mission in the region had been detained and subjected to a virginity test.

The threat of a virginity test is also used to intimidate. In August 1992 a 43-year-old Kurdish woman and her 19-year-old daughter were arrested while they were attending a funeral in Diyarbakir. They were tortured and interrogated about how they knew the man who had been buried. According to the daughter, "They constantly threatened to take me for virginity control and then to rape me when and if they found I wasn't a virgin".

Forced virginity examinations appear to have been used as a means of punishment. An attorney representing prisoners in Nevsehir Prison, who also worked with the Istanbul Human Rights

Association, told HRW that in April 1993 eight women prisoners were discovered attempting to dig a tunnel with male prisoners: "The prison director ordered the women to be taken for virginity control exams. The women resisted, but were examined nonetheless. The women called the press to protest their treatment. According to the attorney, despite calls for action from these women and the Human Rights Association, no investigation into the women's allegations has been initiated."

The social stigma attached to being forcibly tested for virginity is so great that many women do not report such tests, making it difficult to estimate what numbers are involved.

Forced gynaecological examinations designed to degrade and humiliate women have also been reported in China. Eighteen women members of the Jesus Family arrested in Duoyigou, Shandong province, in 1992, are among many women arrested during China's crack-down on independent religious groups in recent years. Several of these women are now serving sentences of up to three years' "re-education through labour", an administrative punishment which is imposed without charge or trial.

The Jesus Family is a community of Chinese Christians in Shandong province which is not recognized by the government-sanctioned Three-Self Patriotic Movement of Protestant Churches of China. In mid-1992 public security officers raided the Duoyigou community of the Jesus Family, destroying their buildings and arresting 37 people. According to testimony received by Amnesty International, while in police custody women members of the Jesus Family were forced to have gynaecological examinations in the presence of the male warden of the county detention centre:

> *"[He] said if we did not take off our underwear ourselves, he would order two male staff members to take off our underwear for us. Since most of us women were unmarried and young, we all felt furious and we cried with rage ... the head of the county Public Security Bureau humiliated us further by saying that if any of us were found pregnant, we would be sent to the hospital and forced to have an abortion."*

At risk in law

In November 1990 Saudi women demonstrated for the right to drive, traditionally denied them. Dozens of women drove in convoy along one of Riyadh's main streets. Their protest was stopped by police who detained 49 of the women until male members of their families signed an undertaking that they would not defy the ban again. Many of the women, who came from wealthy backgrounds, lost their jobs after their protest. A week later the Ministry of the Interior introduced legislation banning female drivers, thereby turning custom and practice into law.

All over the world women are discriminated against in civil and criminal justice systems. Few countries can claim that they honour the principle that all shall be equal before the law when the victims or the defendants (or sometimes even the lawyers) are women.

In Iraq a decree passed in 1990 gave men the legal right to act as judge and executioner, by killing female relatives for "reasons of honour." The decree was rescinded within two months; whether the implicit message about women's human rights in Iraq passed equally swiftly into history is another matter. In Egypt men may be excused for killing their wives, if they find them in the act of adultery. Egyptian women who kill adulterous husbands face the death penalty.

In some countries, however, the law goes further; it does not only discriminate, it provides for particularly cruel, inhuman and degrading punishments for offences committed by women.

Women who fail to follow the strict dress laws in Iran risk arrest and flogging. Hundreds of women were arrested for this reason during a nationwide crack-down on "vice and social corruption" in June 1993. The main target of the crack-down was women who were not covered with the *chador*. Most were released shortly after arrest but a number were sentenced to be flogged. The punishment for infringing the dress code is 74 lashes. The following month the head of the judiciary urged government officials to fire women staff who flouted the dress code at work. As part of the crack-down, the government set up Special Patrols with powers to set up road-blocks, stop and search vehicles and seize them if female passengers were in violation of the dress laws.

In March 1991 the Sudanese military government introduced a penal code which provides cruel, inhuman and degrading treatments, such as amputation and flogging. While few amputations have since been carried out, hundreds of people, many of them women, have been flogged. The 1991 penal code defines a wide variety of offences which are punishable by flogging: prostitution is punishable by up to 100 lashes, wearing clothing contrary to public decency is punishable by up to 40 lashes.

Many of the hundreds of women who have been flogged are from the poor and impoverished displaced population in and around major cities. Many displaced southern women brew and sell alcohol as a way of supporting themselves and their families in the squatter camps. While strictly within the terms of the law non-Muslims who make or sell alcohol are not liable to be flogged, there are many reports of non-Muslim women being flogged for alcohol-related offences. The penal code makes brewing, selling and consuming alcoholic drinks punishable by up to 40 lashes. In one three-day period in early 1993, seven non-Muslim women, two of them pregnant, were given 40 lashes each after being arrested for brewing alcohol in al-Mayo squatter settlement in Khartoum.

Specific offences within the penal code, and provisions within certain by-laws, such as those which define standards of dress, have been interpreted in ways which particularly affect women and have led to them being flogged. The Penal Code 1991 does not prescribe any particular form of dress, but Section 152 defines the offence of wearing an outfit that is obscene or contrary to public morals. In December 1991 the Governor of Khartoum issued general guidelines which included keeping the entire body covered and ensuring the attire is sufficiently loose and opaque to conceal the shape of the body. Trousers or buttoned shirts uncovered by a long loose garment are not regarded as appropriate. Additionally, women should not wear perfume, jewellery or make-up. Although the terms of Section 152 are ambiguous about whether it applies to non-Muslims, and some non-Muslims have been convicted under it, it has been particularly applied to Muslim women. A non-Muslim woman living in Omdurman was fined and sentenced to 35 lashes after being arrested in late 1991 for wearing trousers:

> *"I paid them their fine but I refused to take the lashes. So at once the judge called a policeman from outside who took his whip and suddenly lashed me on my back. I was boiling with anger so I reacted badly. I grabbed the whip and twisted it. Then two or three policemen grabbed me and tied my hands to my back ... they lashed me with my hands tied to my back.*
>
> *"Before they finished I was crying and shouting 'Jesus'. At once the judge stopped the man from lashing and asked*

> *me, 'Why did you say Jesus? Is this a church for you to say Jesus? ... This is not the place of Christians. You must not say Jesus again.' Then he said, 'Add on another five lashes.'*
>
> *"After I received 40 lashes, because I was angry, I gave him a venomous look. He noticed and gave me another five lashes."*

Women who do not conform to the dress code risk arrest on suspicion of other offences connected with public morality which are also punishable by flogging. In late 1991 a non-Muslim Ethiopian woman working as a domestic servant in Gereif was arrested while on an errand for her employers, on suspicion that she was a prostitute. The officer was alone and in plain clothes and so she resisted the arrest because she suspected he might have been seeking to abduct and rape her. She reported being held overnight at a police station with 15 other women arrested while trying to get transport home. They were subjected to verbal abuse and humiliation by the police officers. At the Public Order Court next day they were all accused of being prostitutes:

> *"The judge, when he came, just took our names one by one. And after that he gave 40 lashes for each. He did not advise us, he did not even ask us the reasons we were there. He just sat down for some time, he took our names and after that he gave 40 lashes each. And we saw that the policemen who were looking through the doors, through the windows, were laughing at us."*

In February 1993 Pakistan's Federal *Shari'a* Court suspended a sentence of death by stoning imposed by a lower court on Nasreen, a 35-year-old woman, for adultery.

During the trial, Nasreen told the lower court that her first husband had repudiated her and told her that this was sufficient to make the divorce final under Islamic law. When she later married another man, Ghulam Jaffer, her first husband accused them of adultery and unlawful marriage. The couple were found guilty. Nasreen was sentenced to serve five years in prison before being stoned to death. Ghulam Jaffer was sentenced to public flogging. They appealed to the Federal *Shari'a* Court, which suspended the judgment pending a hearing by a full bench of the *Shari'a* Court and released the couple.

Nasreen and her husband had been sentenced under the

Hudood Ordinance, promulgated in 1979 by the then martial law authorities, as part of a program of "Islamization". Under the Ordinance the offence of *zina* — extra-marital sexual relations — carries penalties of public flogging, imprisonment, or stoning to death.

In 1988 two women who had been raped by police at Nawan Kot Police Station in Lahore had a case registered against them for the offence of *zina*. An official inquiry confirmed they had been raped and that the charges were false. Although the Lahore High Court ordered a criminal case to be registered against the police officers responsible, no action is known to have been taken.

In a rape case the onus of proof falls on the victim. If a woman fails to prove that she did not consent to intercourse the court may convict her of committing *zina*. Despite the risk that their case will fail, women who have been raped are frequently forced to register the attack and undergo judicial proceedings. A woman who remains silent and is later discovered to have had extra-marital sex — by becoming pregnant, or being found to have lost her virginity — runs the risk of being charged with *zina*. In Karachi Central Court alone, about 15 per cent of rape trials reportedly result in the woman who brought the case being charged with *zina* and imprisoned.[13]

In 1993 Taslima Nasrin, a feminist Bangladeshi author, published *Lajja* (Shame), a book about the persecution of Bangladesh's Hindu minority. The book, now banned in Bangladesh, caused a storm of protest and led to Islamist groups offering a reward of 100,000 taka (US$2,000) to anyone who killed Taslima Nasrin. Thousands of people marched through Dhaka, demanding her death. In June 1994 a warrant was issued for Taslima Nasrin's arrest after she was alleged to have insulted the religious feelings of Muslims by suggesting the Koran should be revised during an interview with an Indian newspaper. She says that she was misquoted. In August 1994 Taslima Nasrin fled Bangladesh in fear of her life.

Taslima Nasrin is among a number of people and organizations who have had *fatwas* pronounced against them as Islamist activities in Bangladesh intensify. The government has largely failed to protect such people from death threats. Journalists reporting on Taslima Nasrin and Islamist activities have been attacked. Foreign and Bangladeshi non-governmental organizations which train women to become self-supporting have also been threatened

Taslima Nasrin, a feminist Bangladeshi author forced to flee the country in fear of her life after publishing a book about the persecution of Bangladesh's Hindu minority.
© AP/*Pavel Rahman*

Women from the Women's Development Forum in the Bangla Motor Area, Dhaka, in Bangladesh protest against the fatwas against women © The Daily Star

or have had their offices set on fire or bombed. Islamists assert that these organizations alienate women from their "proper" social roles and Islamic life-styles. In March 1994 a senior Islamic cleric issued orders to 10 men to divorce their wives because they worked for non-governmental organizations. Sixty other families were declared social outcasts for their involvement with foreign aid agencies. Schools and women's health and family planning centres have been subject to arson attacks.

Bangladeshi women are particularly at risk in areas where local village councils controlled by Islamists have set themselves up as enforcers of Islamic law. In the past three years, these councils, known as *salish*, which are not part of the judicial system and have no legal authority, have ordered the execution, torture or ill-treatment of women.

In January 1993 a young woman, Noorjahan Begum, was publicly stoned in Chatakchara, a village in Sylhet district. A *salish* had declared that her second marriage was illegal under Islamic law (her first marriage had broken down and had been dissolved), and that she had therefore committed adultery. Noorjahan and her husband Motaleb were sentenced to death by stoning; Noorjahan's parents were sentenced to be publicly flogged with 50 lashes, as the *salish* considered them partly responsible for the "un-Islamic" second marriage.

Immediately after the verdict, Noorjahan was buried in the ground up to her chest, then villagers began throwing stones at her. She died a few hours later; according to some reports she survived the stoning but committed suicide. Motaleb, her husband, reportedly survived.

The government took action in this case. In February 1994 nine men were sentenced to seven years' imprisonment each for their participation in the stoning of Noorjahan Begum. They have appealed against their sentences. Reports of illegal punishments being ordered by village *salish* continue. In January 1994 the Bangladeshi newspaper *Ajker Kagoj* reported that a *fatwa* had been issued by the imam of a mosque in Begumganj, in Noahkali district. The victim, a young woman named Dulali, was to be caned 101 times in public for allegedly having an adulterous relationship with a local married businessman. According to the report, the local police chief prevented the verdict from being carried out, but criminal charges were not brought against any members of the *salish*.

At risk in society

The majority of women who fall victim to human rights violations come from the poorest and most vulnerable groups in society: homeless women in the world's great cities, indigenous women, women belonging to socially disadvantaged groups such as the Scheduled Castes and Tribes in India, ethnic minority women, women in immigrant communities, women who are criminalized because of their sexual orientation.

> *"At Yebyu camp I was made to dig bunkers, latrines, look after the vegetable garden, fetch water for them, clean their uniforms ... when we couldn't manage the jobs — especially the digging, that was very hard — we were beaten by the soldiers. At night we had to sleep in the same place with the soldiers. The young women — I was the only old one — were forced to sleep with the soldiers, all night."*

The speaker is a 55-year-old Muslim woman in Myanmar (Burma) who was forced to stay at an army camp in March 1993. She is one of hundreds of women who have been abducted and forced to work for Myanmar's army, known as the *tatmadaw*, in recent years.

Myanmar's security forces have been responsible for gross human rights violations against the country's ethnic minorities groups since 1984. The *tatmadaw* continues to torture, ill-treat and kill members of ethnic minorities, including the Karen, Mon, Shan and Kaya groups. Villagers have been seized and forced to work as porters or unpaid labourers; some have been severely ill-treated and many have been killed.

Women and children often bear the brunt of forced labour for the army, mainly because they have been left behind when the men flee the villages in the face of *tatmadaw* abuses. In addition to beatings and poor conditions, women are at risk of rape by troops during their detention as porters and forced labourers.

One young woman who was seized with her aunt described to Amnesty International the general conditions during the month she was detained as a porter:

> *"I was taken from my village with 10 other local girls in November 1992 ... we were collected together with another 100 villagers ... all of whom were women ... we were given very little to eat, and even then it was unhusked rice, so we*

had to spend hours taking the husk off with our fingers. My aunt died, from starvation and fever. I had to bury her myself. She was so thin, no flesh at all."

Amnesty International also interviewed several women who were forced to work on roads, including a 20-year-old Karen Muslim woman with three children who had to guard the road from insurgents from Pa'an to Hlaingbwe for one month in March 1993. She described her duties there:

"... All day and all night we were meant to stay awake and watch the road ... Sometimes soldiers would drive along the road to check that we were awake. If they found us sleeping they made us hop like a frog between one tree and the next, or would give us other kinds of punishments ... One woman, who was very old, maybe 80, died after about 10 days of sitting under the tree — it was very hot ... Another two children, about 10 and 12, also died."

Ethnic minorities and disadvantaged social groups have been

A Roma family near Kardjali, Bulgaria. In several Central European countries Roma people have been singled out for illegal detention, torture and ill-treatment. © Melanie Friend/FORMAT

the target of official violence across the world. Economically disadvantaged and marginalized by cultural and linguistic factors, they often have little access to state institutions through which they could seek redress. Sometimes access to redress is blocked by state agents charged with protecting them; often, instead of protection, these women meet official abuse.

In Bulgaria, Hungary, Romania and the Slovak Republic, Roma people have been singled out for illegal detention, torture and ill-treatment.

In November 1993 a group of some 20 Roma women, men and children were detained by a police officer and three armed men for illegally picking grapes near the village of Glushnik in Bulgaria's Sliven region. They were locked in a pigsty overnight. The following morning church bells summoned the villagers to the pigsty where the Roma were held. Three of the Roma managed to escape; the others were taken out of the pigsty one by one and tied to a metal fence with their hands behind their backs. They were then beaten by the police officer, the local mayor and the villagers. While they were being beaten the Roma women were threatened with rape. At noon a police patrol arrived in the village and released the Roma. No action is known to have been taken against those responsible for detaining and beating the Roma.

Police also routinely fail to protect Roma from attacks by civilians. In September 1993 racial violence erupted in the Romanian village of Hadareni. Three Roma men were killed and over a dozen houses set alight by a crowd of villagers, while a squad of 45 police officers looked on. Most of the Roma community fled the village. When some returned later to collect their belongings they were ill-treated and harassed by the police. Among them were two women who wanted to collect some of their livestock. On their way to the village they were attacked and beaten by a police officer who warned them not to come back. In another case of police harassment in November, Maria Moldovan complained to the police about their alleged beating of her son, who was helping to rebuild Roma homes. She was then fined for disturbing the peace "by shouting that her son had been beaten". She has appealed against the fine. In June 1994 she was arrested and imprisoned for two days.

A similar incident occurred in Bulgaria in March 1994, when a group of around 50 right-wing "skinheads" attacked Roma homes in the town of Pleven. Windows were broken and household appliances and furniture set on fire. After an hour the police arrived and stopped the attack but did not arrest any of the "skinheads", although the identity of many of them was well known. Instead, one of the police officers who went to Milka Koleva Marinova's home to inspect the damage beat her and her child with a truncheon.

In May 1993 Hungarian police raided a Roma community in Béke utca in Orkény, about 50 kilometres south of Budapest. The police were investigating a theft from a car belonging to a German tourist. They searched houses and allegedly beat their occupants with rubber truncheons and sprayed them with tear-gas. Radics Mártonné was beaten with truncheons when she came out of her house to see what was happening. Her husband and 13-year-old son Kristian were arrested. Lakatos Lászlóné, a 55-year-old woman, fainted and was taken to hospital after an officer beat her, ripped off her tracheotomy tube and sprayed tear-gas in her face. Fehér Péterné, who was five months pregnant, tried to protect Lakatos Lászlóné as she lay unconscious. She too was beaten and sprayed with tear-gas. She later required medical treatment for her injuries and miscarried. No action has been reported against the police officers responsible.

Women from a village in Kosovo come to give moral support to an ethnic Albanian man who has been beaten up by the Serbian police. Ethnic minorities and disadvantaged social groups continue to be targets of official violence across the world. © Melanie Friend/FORMAT

At least 15 ethnic Albanian women in Kosovo province of the Republic of Serbia have been beaten and ill-treated by police officers searching for arms. There is a long history of police abuse, principally beatings and other forms of ill-treatment, of ethnic Albanians in the predominantly Albanian-populated province of Kosovo. This takes place against a background of continued confrontation between the Serbian authorities and ethnic Albanians, many of whom refuse to recognize Serbian authority in the province and support demands for secession.

Arms searches have become a prominent feature of policing in Kosovo since the outbreak of armed conflict in the former Yugoslavia in 1991. Over the past year arms searches, often accompanied by ill-treatment, have increased dramatically. They are now conducted on a daily basis, most intensively in border villages and rural areas, but also more generally throughout the province. While most police violence is directed against adult males, women, the elderly, and children have also suffered beatings.

During 1994 a number of incidents were reported of women being beaten by police officers searching for arms. On 17 May police carried out an arms search at the home of Xhevat, Agim and Latif Xhaka in a village near Podujevo. During the search, police officers severely beat a female member of the family, Nazife Xhaka, breaking two of her teeth. At 6am on 31 May, police came to the home of Ilaz and Hamdi Kolludra in Pantina village near Vucitrn to search for arms. During the search they beat 16-year-old Mirvete Kolludra and her father, Ilaz. On 10 June police from Celopek police station searched the home of Halit Berisha in Grabanica. In the course of the search they broke up furniture, burned a hand-embroidered Albanian national flag and beat members of the family, including two women, Hajrije and Miradije Berisha. On 13 June Emine Hyseni and her daughter Lumnije were beaten by police officers at a police station in the village of Klokot near Vitina. Police officers had been looking for Emine's 18-year-old son, Faton Hyseni. Between 6am and 8am on 25 June police searched the home of Hilmi Durmishi in Pristina, looking for his son Rashit, a local activist of the main ethnic Albanian opposition party, the Democratic League of Kosovo (LDK). Rashit was out at the time. During the search police officers beat his wife, Shehide, in front of the children.

Thirteen-year-old Nirmala is a member of one of India's most disadvantaged social groups, the Scheduled Castes and Tribes. In early 1994 her story provoked outrage and protest. She had worked

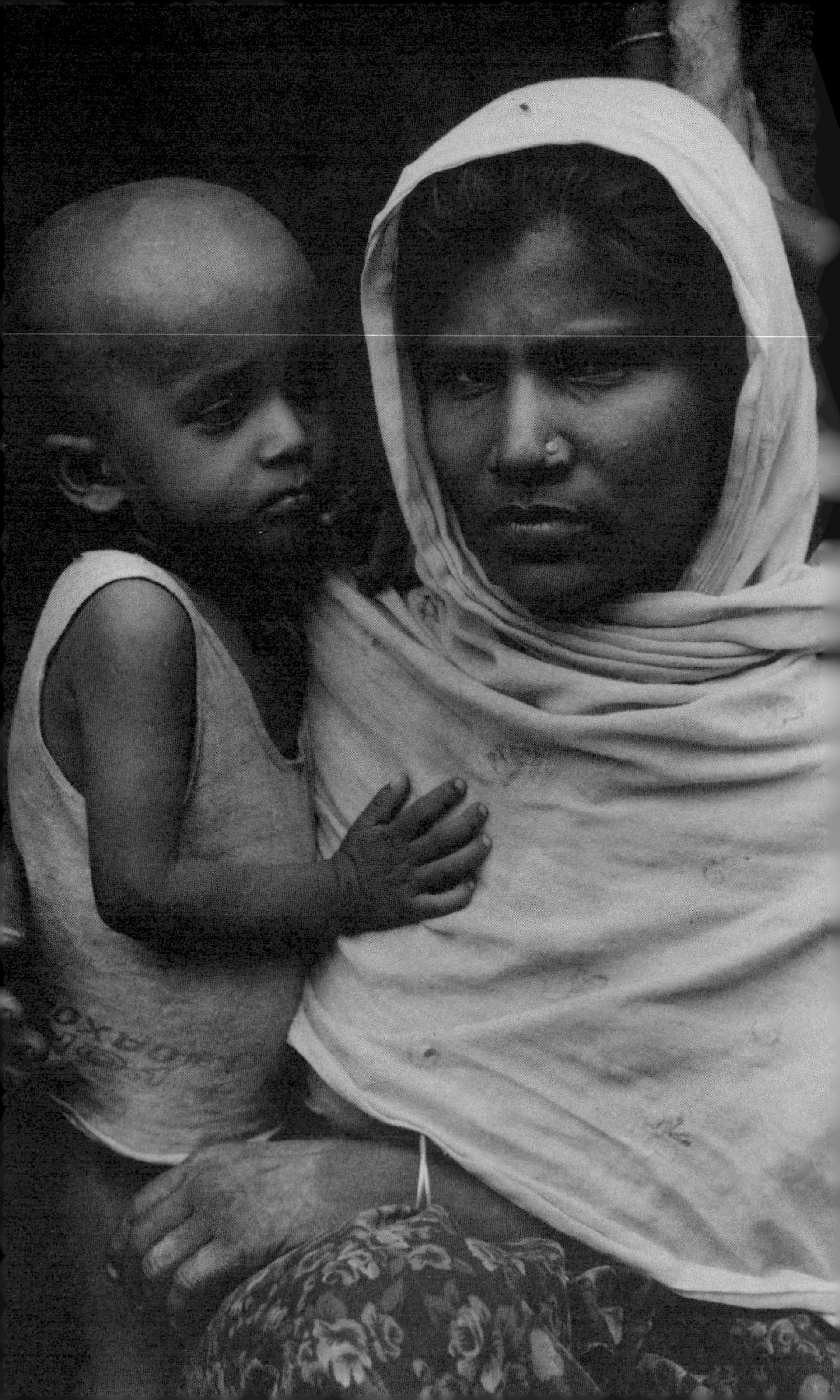

as a maid for about six months, during which time she had been branded with a hot hair-dryer, beaten with iron rods and a rolling pin and bitten by her employers. When her father discovered what was being done to her he took his daughter away and attempted to lodge a complaint with the police. The police refused to register the complaint. He then took his daughter to hospital, where hospital personnel asked the police to register the complaint. Nirmala's father was then summoned to the police station and put under pressure to withdraw the complaint. Instead he approached his member of parliament, who drew public attention to Nirmala's story and demanded action against the police.

Members of the Scheduled Castes and Tribes (known as *dalits*[14] and *adivasis*) are the poorest and most vulnerable groups of people in India. Their special vulnerability has been recognized as requiring extra protection, notably in the Indian Constitution and in the 1988 Scheduled Castes and Scheduled Tribes Act. Women are singled out for special protection under the Act. The degradations they suffer range from gang-rape to being stripped and paraded naked through villages. Despite the Act, official action against those responsible for criminal offences against *dalit* and *adivasi* women is rare. This may be because members of the police force and the army are themselves frequently responsible for raping and otherwise torturing *dalit* and *adivasi* women.

In July 1993 Vijaya, a 17-year-old *adivasi* girl from Athiyur village in Tamil Nadu, was taken to Pondicherry police station to be questioned about a crime of which her cousin was suspected. Afterwards, she said, she was taken to a cow-shed and raped by five police officers for several hours.

When Vijaya was finally allowed to go home she told her mother about the gang-rape. The next morning she and her mother tried to register a complaint but the police refused to record it and sent them away. Only when other villagers protested did the police take the case seriously. The Inspector General of Pondicherry Police announced that there would be an investigation and that if police officers were found guilty of rape, "the severest action" would be taken against them. No action has been reported. However, an

---

Page 104: ***Muslim refugees from Myanmar at the Noyapara refugee camp on the border between Bangladesh and Myanmar. Myanmar's security forces have been responsible for gross human rights violations against the country's minority groups since 1984. © Howard J. Davies***

independent human rights group found substantial evidence to support Vijaya's claim of rape and said the police had covered up their involvement.

In October 1993 a squad of 25 police officers raided a *dalit* village in Jagasinghpur district of Orissa whose inhabitants were in dispute with a local landlord. The night before the raid villagers had prevented the arrest of five people involved in the land dispute, injuring four police officers in the process.

During the raid police officers reportedly gang-raped several women and children at gunpoint in front of their relatives. Police officials denied that women were raped during the raid. However, independent and official investigations found evidence to the contrary. In November 1993 the Chief Minister of Orissa ordered a judicial inquiry into the incident. In September 1994 the inquiry absolved the police of all charges of rape.

Four *dalit* women from Sangrur district, Punjab, were detained in December 1993 and had their foreheads tattooed with the words *jab katri* (female pickpocket) by police officers in Amritsar. The women were arrested at a bus stop and accused of stealing a purse from a tourist. They were detained, illegally, for more than a week, and after their release filed a complaint against the police. This resulted in the harassment of the women and their families, according to the All-India Democratic Women's Association, which visited their village and met their relatives. "The continuing pressure of the police to withdraw the complaint has further terrorized the entire community, many of their women have even left the village."[15] Nevertheless they took their complaint to the Punjab and Haryana High Court, where the judges advised their lawyer to propose adequate compensation for their treatment. In April 1994 the Punjab and Haryana High Court ordered the state government to give the women compensation of Rs 50,000 and to pay for surgery or other treatment to remove the tattoos.

In Europe women of non-European ethnic origin have been the victims of official violence. In July 1993 Moufida Ksouri, a 24-year-old French citizen of Tunisian origin, was returning to France from Italy with three friends. The Italian police checked their identities at the border. Moufida Ksouri was not carrying her identity papers and was taken into the frontier post where two Italian police officers stripped her and then raped her. They then took her to the French border post which was staffed by two border police officers.

One of the officers, a police corporal, allegedly assaulted her in the toilets of the post and forced her to have sexual relations with him.

On 19 July Moufida Ksouri made a formal complaint at the police station in Cannes. She also stated that the police had made racist insults. According to press reports, the General Inspectorate of the National Police was ordered to investigate and a French magistrate indicted both police officers on charges of indecent behaviour. One officer was remanded in custody, the other was freed under judicial control. The detained officer acknowledged that he had had oral sexual relations with Moufida Ksouri, but asserted that she had provoked him. The two Italian officers were also detained and indicted on 6 August 1993. On 14 July 1994 a court in San Remo sentenced them to five years and eight months' imprisonment. At the time of writing, the investigation in France had not concluded.

In the United Kingdom there have been allegations of the cruel, inhuman or degrading treatment of women forcibly deported as illegal immigrants or after being refused asylum. Joy Gardner, a 40-year-old Jamaican woman, was arrested by immigration and police officers for removal from the United

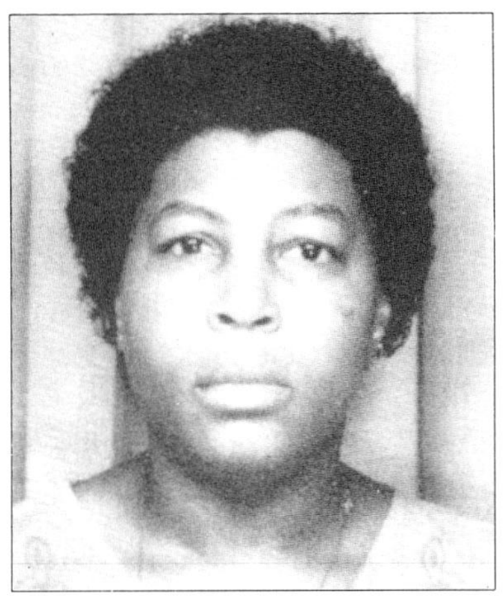

Above: Joy Gardner, who fell into a coma and subsequently died after being bound and gagged by United Kingdom police officers.
© Reuters/Popperfoto
Below: *Joy Gardner's mother and son join a protest outside the local police station after her death on 1 August 1993. © Reuters/Popperfoto*

Kingdom in July 1993. Having been bound and gagged, Joy Gardner collapsed, fell into a coma and was pronounced dead four days later. A storm of protest over her death led to the suspension of the use of the mouth gag in August 1993.

Dorothy Nwokedi, a 31-year-old Nigerian asylum-seeker, and her four-year-old daughter were seized from their home in North London at 6am on 9 July 1993. Dorothy Nwokedi claimed that she was injured by the officials trying to restrain her and take her to the airport and that, once she was on the plane, one official sat on her while others wrapped broad adhesive tape, normally used for securing luggage, around her legs from the knees to the ankles and threatened to use a mouth gag if she did not cooperate. Dorothy Nwokedi alleged that the adhesive tape and handcuffs were not removed until two hours after take-off. The Immigration Service claimed that its own internal investigation had found no evidence of excessive use of force against Dorothy Nwokedi. However, in November 1993, following the investigation into the case, the government banned the use of adhesive tape to restrain deportees.

Allegations of ill-treatment made against immigration officers and private security officers involved in forcible deportations are investigated by the Immigration Service without any independent supervision. In the cases known to Amnesty International, no action has been taken against officials alleged to have ill-treated deportees. Rukhsana Faqir, a 23-year-old Pakistani woman, claimed that the immigration and police officials who arrested her on 29 July 1993 dragged her down the stairs, threw her on a settee and slapped her face. She also stated that although she was suffering from dizziness, headaches and backache as result of the way in which she was arrested no medical treatment was offered. The Home Office claimed that she did receive medical attention and that a police doctor could find no signs of physical injury. The case was investigated by the West Midlands Police, but was not referred to the Police Complaints Authority. The Immigration Service stated that it was satisfied with the investigation and that there were no grounds for any disciplinary action against any of the officers involved. Rukhsana Faqir was deported to Pakistan on 30 December 1993.

Persecution on grounds of sexual orientation

Involvement in a lesbian relationship can cost a woman her life in Iran. Any woman convicted four times of *mosaheqeh* (lesbianism) faces the death penalty. Lesbianism can be proved by the testimony of "four righteous men who might have observed it". A lesser punishment is 100 lashes for each party. In 1993 Iran's former representative at the UN, Rajaie Khorasani, confirmed that homosexuality could be punished by the death penalty. Representing Iran's consultative assembly at an inter-parliamentary symposium in Budapest, he outlined the punishments of *shageh* for homosexuality under *Shi'a* jurisprudence as cleaving into two halves lengthwise, pushing off a cliff, or stoning to death.

Women who are involved in sexual relationships with other women are referred to as lesbians in this report. Lesbians exist in every sector and are members of all groups of society. Through their public actions and organizations, lesbians are often targeted by governments seeking to control their identities and activism. Lesbians face double jeopardy: vulnerable to abuse because they are

Katie Taylor holds a photograph of herself after she had been attacked. Abuses against lesbians are all too often surrounded by silence.
© Donna Binder/Impact Visuals

women, lesbians are further marginalized and stigmatized because of their sexual orientation.

The abuses that lesbians face range from torture, including rape and sexual abuse by government authorities, to arbitrary imprisonment, "disappearance", and extrajudicial execution.

In 1979 Amnesty International affirmed that those imprisoned for advocating lesbian and gay rights would be considered prisoners of conscience and in 1982 the organization condemned the forcible "medical" treatment carried out on people in detention against their will for the purpose of altering their sexual orientation. In 1991 the organization expanded its mandate with regard to work on behalf of imprisoned lesbians and gay men. Amnesty International now considers for adoption anyone who is imprisoned solely because of their homosexuality, including the practice of homosexual acts in private between consenting adults.

The abuses lesbians suffer are often surrounded by silence because lesbians themselves frequently do not have access to the resources needed to call attention to ill-treatment. This means that the abuses committed against them are even more difficult to monitor and punish. These women may be afraid to publicize the abuse, since when the abuses are made public, lesbians often face the additional hardship of being stigmatized and thus unable to gather popular support. Further, because many lesbians are unable to be public about their sexual identity for fear of reprisal, they suffer without public acknowledgment that harm has occurred.

This silence and invisibility often extends even to groups working for women's rights, who hesitate to speak out against human rights abuses perpetrated against lesbians for fear of being further marginalized. In addition, because of the international community's failure to see lesbian and gay rights as human rights, abuses against them frequently go unreported by local, national and international human rights organizations.

The lack of documentation of abuses against lesbians leads to a context in which further abuses may occur. For example, lesbians have sometimes been denied political asylum on the basis of their sexual orientation because they were unable to show documented abuses against lesbians in their countries. This is partly due to a failure by human rights groups to document these abuses, and partly because while many laws are explicit only in reference to gay men, in practice they provide the context for abuses against lesbians. Lesbians, along with gay men, have historically been persecuted through laws that criminalize sexual behaviour between consenting adults of the same sex (commonly referred to as "sodomy laws") even when such behaviour occurs in private.

In many parts of the world homosexuality remains illegal. Sections of the Criminal Code of the Australian state of Tasmania allow for the prosecution and imprisonment of consenting adults who engage in homosexual acts in private. In the USA, consensual homosexual acts in private are punishable by imprisonment in five states: Arkansas, Kansas, Missouri, Montana, and Tennessee. The penalties in these states range from 30 days' to 10 years' imprisonment.

In Romania, sexual acts between consenting gay men or lesbians are outlawed under Article 200 of the Romanian Penal Code. This law provides one to five years' imprisonment for anyone convicted of "having sexual relations with a person of the same sex".

In recent months, the Romanian Parliament has been debating changing Article 200. Some of the proposed changes could be

Amnesty International demonstration for gay rights in the USA

interpreted to criminalize an even broader set of actions, while other proposals would narrow the proscription against homosexual conduct to include only sex which occurs "in public". The debate within the parliament demonstrated the precarious situation for lesbians and gay men in Romania, with members of parliament stating that homosexuality is an "aberration", or a "genetic accident". Although gay men are most frequently targeted for abuse under Article 200, the law itself proscribes homosexual acts between both men and women and is thus a continuing threat to lesbians. Proposals to revise Article 200 are still being debated by the Romanian Chamber of Deputies.

The criminalization of sexual acts not only means that lesbians and gay men face a constant threat of prosecution but also that their legal rights are indirectly affected. In the state of Georgia, a teenager was sentenced to death for murder in 1981. During the trial allegations concerning her involvement in homosexual acts were presented to the jury in an inflammatory manner. Janice Buttrum, who was 17 years old at the time of the crime, was described in the press before her trial as a "bisexual sadist". A psychologist appearing for the state testified, although he had not interviewed Janice Buttrum, that she was a sexual sadist and would commit other violent sexual acts in the future (Janice Buttrum had only one previous conviction for a minor offence, not involving sexual violence). Her death sentence was commuted to life imprisonment on appeal, on the grounds that she had not received a fair hearing.

In June 1992 the Nicaraguan Government amended the country's Penal Code to provide that "anyone who induces, promotes, propagandizes or practises in scandalous form sexual intercourse between persons of the same sex commits the crime of sodomy and shall incur one to three years' imprisonment". This amendment could allow imprisonment of adults who engage in consensual homosexual conduct in private; Amnesty International would consider these people to be prisoners of conscience. The organization is concerned about the wording of this law and fears that those involved in the non-violent advocacy of homosexual rights could also be imprisoned under Article 204 for "promoting" homosexual acts. Gay and lesbian activists, fearing prosecution under Article 204, presented an appeal to the Supreme Court challenging the law as unconstitutional. In March 1994 the Court rejected the appeal. Although the law has not yet been applied, the Supreme Court's decision opens the way for its application.

In addition to legislation which proscribes homosexual acts, laws regarding public behaviour and morality may be used to target lesbians. In Greece, in November 1991 Irene Petropoulu, the chief editor of the gay and lesbian magazine *Amphi*, was sentenced to five months' imprisonment and a 50,000-drachma fine for a comment she had published in an issue of the magazine. The comment, in the classified section, asked why so many homosexual and heterosexual men were interested in corresponding with lesbians. The court ruled that the comment offended "public feelings of decency and sexual morals and cannot be considered to be a work of art and science". Irene Petropoulu appealed against her sentence and was acquitted by the Athens appeal court in September 1993.

'Guilty by association' — relatives as victims

Shin Sook Ja, a 50-year-old radio announcer, and her two daughters, Oh Hae Won, 17, and Oh Kyu Won, 14, have spent years in detention centres in North Korea. They were detained in November 1986 shortly after Shin Sook Ja's husband, Oh Kil Nam, requested political asylum in Germany. He has not been able to contact them or obtain official confirmation of their whereabouts since 1986. In 1989 they were believed to be held in a "re-education through labour" centre in Hamgyoung South Province. In 1994 the North Korean Government stated that Shin Sook Ja was not detained. However, attempts by Amnesty International and others to contact her remained unsuccessful.

Women are often detained, tortured, held hostage and sometimes even killed because their relatives or people they are associated with are connected to political opposition groups, or are wanted by the authorities.

Djamilah Abubakar was 24 years old when she was killed in Aceh, a province in northern Sumatra where Indonesian Government forces have faced armed political opposition for many years. Djamilah Abubakar had been hounded by the military for two years because they suspected her husband, a fisherman named Mohammad Jasin bin Pawang Piah, was a member of the opposition *Aceh Merdeka*. Djamilah Abubakar fled from one village to another, pursued by the military. In March 1991 she was visited by her husband. Within days soldiers seized her and took her away. Her corpse was found later, lying beside a road. Her head was smashed and she had been shot.

As the security forces crack down on the illegal Islamic movement *al-Nahda* (Renaissance) in Tunisia, women have been randomly punished by the authorities because of their relationship to men in jail or wanted by the authorities. When the crack-down started, in 1990, many activists went into hiding and later fled the country. As a result, the security forces detained their wives and female relatives in order to extract information on their whereabouts and to put pressure on the men to give themselves up. Wives of detainees, especially before their trial, were also harassed to extract information about their husbands' political activities. Their homes were regularly visited, especially at night, by members of the security forces, who searched the houses and confiscated possessions without showing any search warrant or giving any receipt.

Wives and other relatives of wanted men have reported that they were frequently threatened and sometimes ill-treated by being pushed or hit by the Tunisian security forces. As a follow-up to these visits women relatives were subsequently repeatedly summoned and taken in for questioning at police stations. Scores of these women have testified that during their time in detention they were tortured, beaten, undressed, sexually abused and threatened with rape. Most were released within hours or, in a few cases, days.

Wives and relatives of Tunisian Islamist political prisoners have fared little better. Wives are often prevented from visiting their husbands on the pretext that their ID cards bear their maiden name only (previously marriage certificates were always accepted as proof); they have to wait for months for a new ID card to be issued, during which time they cannot visit their husbands. Relatives of prisoners or of activists who have left the country, including women, have lost their jobs or their business licence, or have been evicted from their homes. Wives of Islamist prisoners are constantly arrested and interrogated about how they survive (since many have lost their jobs). They, and anyone who has given them financial assistance, face imprisonment on charges of illegal collection of funds. Women are not allowed to wear the headscarf (*hidjab*) when they visit their husbands in prison. Women have also been detained and harassed for passing information about human rights violations to human rights organizations, including Amnesty International.

In May 1994 Amnesty International interviewed several women imprisoned in the Chiclayo Women's Prison in Peru's Lambayeque department. At the time there were 83 women in the prison, 48 of whom were there for "terrorist" offences. More than half of the women interviewed had been forced under torture to "confess" to the accusations against them. Almost all were peasants who came from remote areas in the north of Peru and most were illiterate. They could not read the police statement they were signing or marking with their fingerprints. Many had been arrested solely because their relatives or associates were suspected of involvement with the armed opposition; some were in prison after being denounced.

Victoria Zumaeta Arista is a 37-year-old peasant woman with seven children from a small hamlet in Utcubamba province, Amazonas department. She is also a prisoner of conscience, currently serving a five-year sentence after being convicted of a "terrorist" offence in September 1993. Victoria Zumaeta is in prison solely because her son-in-law had been a member of the clandestine armed opposition group Túpac Amaru Revolutionary Movement (MRTA). Under torture she was forced to state that she knew of her son-in-law's activities and that she herself had collaborated with the MRTA.

Darnilda Pardavé Trujillo spent 13 months in prison charged with "terrorism" solely because her sister was a well-known armed opposition leader. A 38-year-old psychologist, she was first arrested in June 1991, but released after two weeks for lack of evidence. However, the judge who dealt with her case stated in his report:

> *"Even if it is certain from the police investigations that she does not belong to the Shining Path leadership, nor to the rest of its components, even more that no subversive material was found in her possession ... it must also be taken into account that, being the sister of Yovanka Pardavé Trujillo who is awaiting trial, and there being a close connection with the latter, one cannot rule out the possibility that she is familiar with the terrorist actions that her sister will carry out, collaborating with her in an indirect way."*

A few months later, in May 1992, Darnilda Pardavé's sister was killed by the security forces at the Miguel Castro-Castro Prison in Canto Grande along with at least 35 other inmates during an operation by the authorities to reimpose control over prison wings run by Shining Path.

Darnilda Pardavé was arrested again in October 1992, during a mass round-up of people suspected of links with Shining Path.

She was held in Chorrillos, a high-security prison for women accused of "terrorism", in Lima, Peru's capital city. Independent human rights monitors have estimated that at least 60 of the 360 prisoners in Chorrillos are innocent of any involvement with the armed opposition. Darnilda Pardavé was released at the end of October 1993. Shortly afterwards, Amnesty International received this letter:

> *"Your letter arrived on 29 October, the day I was released! ... Thank you for all your support. Your message ... has cheered me up and given me strength during very difficult times. I hope you continue this extraordinary and beautiful work. It contributes to the freedom of many innocent people in prison. Take care of yourself and take care of your family. Give them as much love as you have given me."*

4

Fifteen steps to protect women's human rights

Human rights for women, as for all individuals, are protected in international law. Yet women suffer the full range of human rights violations known to the modern world. Women and girl-children also face human rights violations solely or primarily because of their sex.

The international community can play a decisive role in protecting human rights through vigilant and concerted action. Important steps towards protecting women's human rights worldwide include documenting human rights violations, publicizing these as widely as possible and campaigning to press government authorities for an end to the abuses. Governments which fail to protect fundamental human rights should be confronted with the full force of international condemnation.

Armed political groups should also take steps to prevent abuses of the human rights of women and girl-children.

Amnesty International's 15-point program to protect women from human rights violations contains recommendations which address abuses primarily suffered by women, and the range of human rights violations that women have experienced along with men and children. The recommendations focus on the specific areas of Amnesty International's expertise and aim to complement and contribute to the efforts of others working on women's rights issues.

The campaign to protect women's human rights will have to be waged on the same fronts and the same issues as that to protect everyone's human rights. Some human rights violations, however, require specific action to protect women in particular. The recommendations below reflect the breadth of the campaign.

1 Recognize that women's human rights are universal an indivisible

- The Platform for Action to be adopted by the Fourth UN Worl Conference on Women must reflect the commitment made b governments in the Vienna Declaration and Programme o Action of the 1993 UN World Conference on Human Rights tha "[t]he human rights of women and of the girl-child are a inalienable, integral and indivisible part of universal huma rights".

2 Ratify and implement international treaties for the protection o human rights

- Governments should ratify international legal instrument which provide for the protection of the human rights o women and girl-children, such as:

— the International Covenant on Civil and Political Rights (ICCPR) and its two Optional Protocols;
— the International Covenant on Economic, Social and Cultural Rights;
— the Convention against Torture and Other Cruel, Inhuman or Degrading Treatment or Punishment;
— the Convention on the Elimination of All Forms of Discrimination against Women;
— the Convention on the Rights of the Child;
— the Convention and Protocol relating to the Status of Refugees.

- Governments should also ratify regional standards which protect the human rights of women and girl-children.

- Governments who have already ratified these instruments should examine any limiting reservations, with a view to withdrawing them. This is particularly important in the case of the Convention on the Elimination of All Forms of Discrimination against Women, where the commitment of many governments is seriously undermined by the extent of their reservations.

- Governments should take due account of non-treaty instruments such as the Vienna Declaration and Programme of Action and the Declaration on the Elimination of Violence against Women.

Governments should ensure that reports to treaty-monitoring bodies include detailed information on the situation of women and girl-children.

3 Eradicate discrimination, which denies women human rights

- Governments should recognize that discrimination against women, including lesbians and girl-children, is a key contributory factor to human rights abuse such as torture, including rape and other forms of custodial violence. Governments should initiate a plan of action against such discrimination.

- Governments should ensure that women are treated equally in law; a woman's evidence should have the same weight as a man's in all judicial proceedings and women should not receive harsher penalties than a man would for the same offence.

- Where it is alleged that discrimination in the administration of justice contributes to human rights violations against women an independent commission should be appointed to investigate and make recommendations to rectify the situation.

4 Safeguard women's human rights during armed conflict

- Stop torture, including rape, "disappearances" and extrajudicial executions.

- Take special steps to prevent rape during armed conflict, often the context for violent sexual abuse of women and girl-children. Bring government agents responsible for rape to justice.

- The UN should ensure that personnel deployed in UN peace-keeping and other field operations observe the highest standards of humanitarian and human rights law and receive information on local cultural traditions. They should respect the rights and dignity of women at all times, both on and off duty. Human rights components of UN field operations should include experts in the area of violence against women, including rape and sexual abuse, to ensure that prisons and places of detention where women are held are clearly identified and properly investigated and that victims of rape and other custodial violence have suitable and confidentia facilities to meet investigators who are specially trained an experienced in this area.

5 **Stop rape, sexual abuse and other torture and ill-treatment by government agents and paramilitary auxiliaries**

- Take effective steps to prevent rape, sexual abuse and othe torture and ill-treatment in custody.
- Conduct prompt, thorough and impartial investigations into al reports of torture or ill-treatment. Any law-enforcement agen responsible for such acts, or for encouraging or condoning them, should be brought to justice.
- Any form of detention or imprisonment and all measures affecting the human rights of detainees or prisoners should be subject to the effective control of a judicial authority.
- All detainees should have access to family members and legal counsel promptly after arrest and regularly throughout their detention and/or imprisonment.
- The authorities should record the duration of any interrogation, the intervals between interrogations, and the identity of the officials conducting each interrogation and other persons present.
- Female guards should be present during the interrogation of female detainees and prisoners, and should be solely responsible for carrying out any body searches of female detainees and prisoners to reduce the risk of rape and other sexual abuses. There should be no contact between male guards and female detainees and prisoners without the presence of a female guard.
- Female detainees and prisoners should be held separately from male detainees and prisoners.
- All detainees and prisoners should be given the opportunity to have a medical examination promptly after admission to the place of custody and regularly thereafter. They should also have the right to be examined by a doctor of their choice.
- A medical examination, by a female doctor wherever possible, should be provided immediately for any woman in custody

who alleges she has been raped. This is a crucial measure in obtaining evidence for legal prosecution.

- Victims of rape and sexual abuse and other torture or ill-treatment in custody should be entitled to fair and adequate compensation and appropriate medical care.

6 **Prevent "disappearances" and extrajudicial executions by government agents and compensate the victims**

- Conduct prompt, thorough and impartial investigations into all reports of "disappearances", extrajudicial executions and deaths in custody and bring to justice those responsible.

- Ensure that the commission of a "disappearance" or extrajudicial execution, or causing the death of a prisoner in custody, is a criminal offence, punishable by sanctions commensurate with the gravity of the practice.

- Inform families immediately of any arrest and keep them informed of the whereabouts of the detainee or prisoner at all times.

- Make available judicial remedies (such as *habeas corpus* and *amparo*) to enable lawyers and relatives to locate prisoners and obtain the release of anyone who has been arbitrarily detained.

- Prevent detention or imprisonment other than in official, known detention centres, a list of which should be widely publicized.

- Order forensic investigations into killings and deaths in custody to be carried out promptly and thoroughly by independent qualified personnel.

- Provide fair and adequate redress to relatives of victims of "disappearance", extrajudicial execution and death in custody, including financial compensation.

- The civil status of women whose relatives have "disappeared" should not be penalized. Identity cards, travel documents, other official papers and state benefits should be made available to women whose relatives have "disappeared".

Edméia da Silva Euzébio, mother of a "disappeared" youth in Brazil, who was murdered in January 1993. Prompt, thorough and impartial investigations must be initiated into all reports of "disappearances", extrajudicial executions and deaths in custody. © Jaime Silva/Enfase

7 Stop persecution because of family connections

- Any woman detained, imprisoned or held hostage solely because of her family connections should be immediately and unconditionally released.

- The practice of killing, abducting, or torturing women in order to bring pressure on their relatives should not be tolerated. Anyone responsible for such acts should be brought to justice.

8 Safeguard the health rights of women in custody

- Provide all women under any form of detention or imprisonment with adequate medical treatment, denial of which can constitute ill-treatment.

- Provide all necessary pre-natal and post-natal care and treatment for women in custody and their infants.

- The imprisonment of a mother and child together must never be used to inflict torture or ill-treatment on either by causing physical or mental suffering. If a child is ever separated from its mother in prison she should be immediately notified and continuously kept informed of its whereabouts and given reasonable access to the child.

- Women in custody should be consulted over arrangements made for the care of their infants.

9 Release all prisoners of conscience immediately and unconditionally

- Release all detainees and prisoners held because of their sex, peaceful political beliefs or activities, ethnic origin, sexual orientation, language or religion.

- No woman should be detained or imprisoned for peacefully attempting to exercise basic rights and freedoms enjoyed by men.

- Governments should review all legislation and practices which result in the detention of women because of their homosexual identity or because of homosexual acts in private between consenting adults.

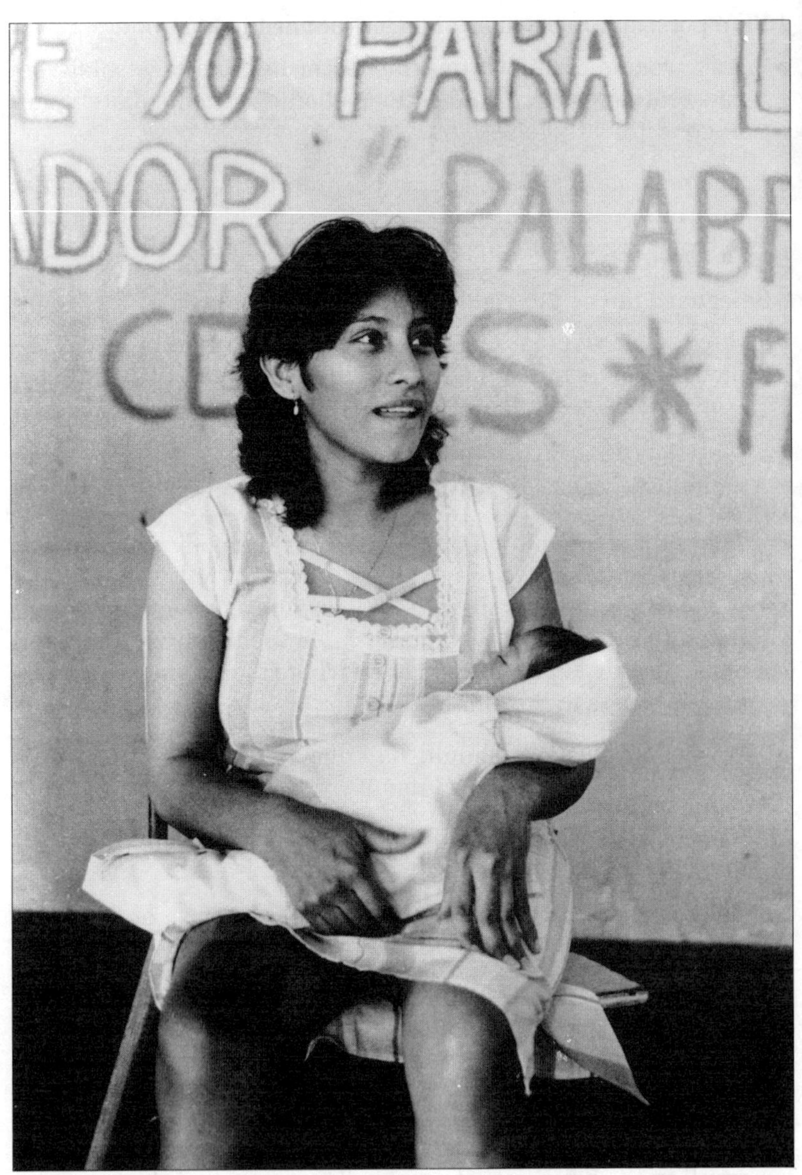

A mother and her young baby born in prison in El Salvador. The imprisonment of a mother and child together must never be used to inflict torture or ill-treatment. © Jenny Matthews

10 **Ensure prompt and fair trials for all political prisoners**

- Stop unfair trials which violate the fundamental rights of political prisoners in all parts of the world.
- Ensure that all political prisoners charged with a criminal offence receive a prompt and fair trial by a competent, independent and impartial tribunal.
- Ensure that all political prisoners are treated in accordance with internationally recognized safeguards for fair legal proceedings.

11 **Prevent human rights violations against women refugees and asylum-seekers and displaced women**

- No one should be forcibly returned to a country where she or he can reasonably be expected to be imprisoned as a prisoner

Tadjik women flee their village near Kumsagor, 100 miles south of Dushanbe, scene of fighting between pro-government and opposition forces. Every woman refugee or asylum-seeker must be given the opportunity of an individual hearing, and not regarded as merely being part of her family.
© Associated Press

of conscience, tortured (including by being raped), "disappeared" or executed.

- Governments should remove all barriers, whether in law or administrative practice, to women seeking political asylum on the basis of persecution based on sexual identity.
- Every woman refugee or asylum-seeker should be given the opportunity of an individual hearing, and should not be regarded as merely being part of her family.
- Governments should take measures to protect women's physical safety and integrity by preventing torture, including rape, and ill-treatment of refugee women and asylum-seekers in the country of asylum. Other forms of sexual abuse/exploitation, such as extorting sexual favours for commodities, must be prevented.
- Governments should thoroughly and impartially investigate human rights violations committed against refugees and asylum-seekers in the country of asylum, and bring to justice those responsible.
- In procedures for the determination of refugee status governments should provide interviewers trained to be sensitive to issues of gender and culture, as well as to recognize the specific protection needs of women refugees and asylum-seekers. Those who may have suffered sexual violence should be treated with particular care, by ensuring that their cases are handled by female staff.
- Women refugees and asylum-seekers should have equal access to procedures for voluntary repatriation, to ensure that those wishing to return are able do to so and to protect those who do not wish to return from *refoulement*.

12 **Abolish the death penalty**

- Governments should abolish the death penalty and stop judicial executions.
- All death sentences should be commuted.
- Legislation which allows a woman to be put to death for an

offence for which a man would receive a lesser sentence should be abolished.

- In countries which retain the death penalty, the law should provide that executions will not be carried out against pregnant women and new mothers, in conformity with international standards.

13 **Support the work of relevant intergovernmental and non-governmental organizations**

- Governments should publicly state their commitment to ensuring that the intergovernmental bodies which monitor violations of human rights suffered by women, including the UN Commission on Human Rights and its Special Rapporteur on violence against women, the UN Commission on the Status of Women and the Committee on the Elimination of Discrimination against Women (CEDAW), have adequate resources to carry out their task effectively.
- The equal status and human rights of women should be integrated into the mainstream of UN system-wide activity. These issues should be regularly and systematically addressed by the relevant UN bodies and mechanisms.
- Governments should guarantee that women activists and non-governmental organizations working peacefully for the promotion and protection of women's human rights enjoy all rights set out in the Universal Declaration of Human Rights and the ICCPR.
- Governments participating in the Fourth UN World Conference on Women should ensure that the Platform for Action adopted at the Conference protects the fundamental civil, political, economic, social and cultural rights of women, and that the measures it contains are implemented.

14 **Promote women's rights as human rights through official programs of education and training**

- Governments should ensure that all law-enforcement personnel and other government agents receive adequate training on national and international standards which protect the human rights of all women and how to enforce them properly.

A meeting of the Gabriella Women's Organization in the Philippines. Women's non-governmental organizations should be recognized as making an important contribution in the human rights arena. © Brenda Prince/FORMAT

A literacy class in Brazil. Literacy is a vital weapon in the struggle for women's human rights. © Jenny Matthews

- Law-enforcement personnel and other government agents should be instructed that rape of women in their custody is an act of torture and will not be tolerated.

- A special emphasis should be given to education designed to make women aware of their rights and to make society at large conscious of its duty to respect the human rights and fundamental freedoms of women and girl-children. Education into the human rights of women and girl-children should be integrated into all education and training policies at both national and international levels.

- Special steps should be taken to uphold the UN Declaration on the Elimination of Violence against Women. These steps should include a clear prohibition of gender-based violence, whether occurring in public or private life.

- Governments should give high priority in development assistance projects for the implementation of human rights, particularly as they affect women and girl-children. The Commission on Human Rights and its secretariat, the Centre for Human Rights, should also be encouraged to ensure that the human rights of women are always given full attention in projects carried out under the Advisory Services and Technical Assistance program. The Centre for Human Rights should be able to respond fully and promptly to requests for assistance in establishing educational programs to combat gender discrimination.

- Governments and intergovernmental organizations should make available human rights education materials which promote women's rights as human rights. These materials should designed to be understood by the illiterate.

15 **Armed political groups should safeguard women's human rights**

- Armed political groups should also take steps to prevent abuses by their members such as hostage-taking, torture, including rape, ill-treatment, and arbitrary and deliberate killings, and to hold those responsible for such abuses to account.

APPENDIX

Female genital mutilation

"In Africa today, women's voices are being raised against genital mutilations still practised on babies, little girls, and women. These voices belong to a few women who, from the Arabic north to the Horn and across to western Africa, remain closely attached to their identity and heritage, but are prepared to challenge it when traditional practices endanger their lives and their health."[16]

An estimated 110 million women suffer serious, even life-threatening, injuries throughout their adult lives as a result of female genital mutilation, a traditional practice which many underwent as teenagers or children, some even as infants. The scale of the practice is enormous; around two million girls are mutilated every year.

Female genital mutilation occurs in some 20 countries in Africa, parts of Asia and the Middle East, and in immigrant communities in other regions, for example Europe. For many years now, African women have been in the forefront of the campaign to eradicate female genital mutilation. Participants from 20 African countries, as well as representatives of international organizations, attending a 1984 seminar in Dakar on "Traditional Practices Affecting the Health of Women and Children" recommended that the practice be abolished and that "in order to change existing attitudes and practice, strong education programmes should be developed and carried out on a constant basis". In 1994 official campaigns against genital mutilation were launched in Egypt and Tanzania.

Largely as a result of grassroots campaigns, governments in several countries have passed legislation on genital mutilation or made it a criminal offence. Some have launched education and awareness campaigns in an attempt to educate women about the consequences. The practice has also been condemned by international organizations such as the UN Commission on Human Rights, UNICEF and the World Medical Association. Female genital mutilation was addressed by the 1993 UN World Conference on Human Rights.

"The World Conference supports all measures by the United Nations and its specialized agencies to ensure the effective protection and promotion of human rights of the girl-child. The World Conference urges States to repeal existing laws and regulations and remove customs and practices which discriminate against and cause harm to the girl-child."

The World Health Organization, which has advised health professionals not to participate in female genital mutilation since 1982, reiterated its opposition to the practice in May 1994, and urged all member states "to assess the extent to which harmful traditional practices affecting the health of women and children constitute a social and public health problem in any local community or sub-group; to establish national policies and programmes that will effectively, and with legal instruments, abolish female genital mutilation ... [and] to collaborate with national non-governmental groups active in this field, draw upon their experience and expertise, and where such groups do not exist, encourage their establishment".[17]

The UNHCR considers that women claiming refugee status on the grounds that their daughters were at risk of forced genital mutilation and that they themselves faced persecution for opposing the practice, combined with an absence of state protection, come under the protection of the 1951 Convention on the Status of Refugees.

The severity of female genital mutilation varies in different cultures; it involves the removal of part or all of the genital organs — clitoris and labia — and is usually performed by older women in a village or by a traditional birth attendant. There are a few reports of mutilations being carried out by doctors or nurses, or in hospital. Except in hospital, anaesthetics are never used. The child is usually held down by a woman lying underneath her who pins her arms and legs with her own, or by village women.

"The little girl, entirely nude, is immobilized in the sitting position on a low stool by at least three women. One of them with her arms tightly around the little girl's chest; two

others hold the child's thighs apart by force, in order to open wide the vulva. The child's arms are tied behind her back, or immobilized by two other women guests.

"... Then the old woman takes her razor and excises the clitoris. The infibulation follows: the operator cuts with her razor from top to bottom of the small lip and then scrapes the flesh from inside of the large lip. This nymphectomy and scraping are repeated on the other side of the vulva.

"The little girl howls and writhes in pain, although strongly held down. The operator wipes the blood from the wound and the mother, as well as the guests, 'verify' her work, sometimes putting their fingers in. The amount of scraping of the large lips depends upon the 'technical' ability of the operator. The opening left for urine and menstrual blood is minuscule.

"Then the operator applies a paste and ensures the adhesion of the large lips by means of an acacia thorn, which pierces one lip and passes through into the other. She sticks in three or four in this manner down the vulva. These thorns are then held in place either by means of sewing thread, or with horse-hair. Paste is again put on the wound.

"But all this is not sufficient to ensure the coalescence of the large lips; so the little girl is then tied up from her pelvis to her feet: strips of material rolled up into a rope immobilize her legs entirely. Exhausted, the little girl is then dressed and put on a bed. The operation lasts from 15 to 20 minutes according to the ability of the old woman and the resistance put up by the child."[18]

The effects of mutilation are surgically irreversible. They were described by the World Medical Association in a statement of condemnation of female genital mutilation issued in October 1993.

"Depending on the extent of the circumcision, FGM [*female genital mutilation*] *affects the health of women and girls. Research evidence shows the grave permanent damage to health. Acute complications of* FGM *are: haemorrhage, infections, bleeding of adjacent organs, violent pain. Later complications are vicious scars, chronic infections, urologic and obstetric complications and psychological and social problems. FGM has serious consequences for sexuality and how it is experienced. There is a multiplicity of complications during childbirth ..."*[19]

In 1992 Minority Rights Group International, an international human rights research and information unit, published *Female Genital Mutilation: Proposals for Change*, a detailed report on the practice, the issues surrounding it, and how to prevent it. In discussing why female genital mutilation is so strongly defended as a traditional practice, the report states: "the reasons given, as they appear in research papers, interviews and testimonials, fall into four main groups: psycho-sexual, religious, sociological and hygienic". Psycho-sexual reasons include the clitoris being considered an aggressive organ; protection of chastity; the belief that an unexcised women cannot give birth. The operation has been justified on religious grounds as a result of the belief that it is demanded by the Islamic faith (although it is also practised by Catholics, Protestants, Copts, Animists and non-believers in the various countries concerned). The sociological reasons given for female genital mutilation include initiation rites and development into adulthood. Health reasons include the belief that the external female genitalia are "dirty".[20]

Most experts agree that the age of mutilation is becoming younger. Efua Dorkenoo, director of the non-governmental organization Forward International, who has campaigned against the practice for more than a decade, attributes this trend to the increased publicity female genital mutilation has recently received. "As a result, parents are now reducing the age at which their daughters are operated on." This has given rise to grave concern:

"While an adult woman is quite free to submit herself to a ritual or tradition, a child has no formed judgement and does not consent but simply undergoes the operation while she is totally vulnerable. The descriptions available of the reaction of children — panic and shock from extreme pain, biting through the tongue, convulsions, necessity for six adults to hold down an eight-year-old, and death — indicate a practice comparable to torture."[21]

ENDNOTES

[1] *South China Morning Post, AFP*, 21 January 1994

[2] Amnesty International considers anyone detained for their beliefs or because of their ethnic origin, sex, race or language to be a prisoner of conscience, provided they have not used or advocated violence.

[3] Charlotte Bunch, in *Human Rights — the New Consensus*, United Nations High Commissioner for Refugees, Regency Press (Humanity) Ltd, London, 1994

[4] Report on the situation of human rights in the territory of the former Yugoslavia, Tadeusz Mazowiecki. UN ref: E/CN.4/1993/50, p. 19

[5] Presentation at Amnesty International British Section conference on human rights violations against women, April 1994

[6] Ronald D. Crelinsten and Alex P. Schmid (editors), *The Politics of Pain*, Leiden: COMT, 1993, p. 99.

[7] State of the World's Children 1992, UNICEF

[8] *Observer*, 24 July 1994

[9] *The National Law Journal*, New York, 20 September 1993

[10] *Ibid*

[11] HRW/Women's Rights Project, June 1994, Vol. 6, No. 7

[12] *Cumhuriyet*, 24 June 1992

[13] *Eastern Eye*, London, 14 June 1994

[14] The term *dalit* — meaning "oppressed" — has been used to describe militant members of the scheduled castes. It has now gained wider currency and Amnesty International uses it in its broadest sense to describe all members of the scheduled castes, not merely the most militant.

[15] *The Hindustan Times*, New Delhi, 22 January 1994

[16] *Female Genital Mutilation: Proposals for Change*, by Efua Dorkenoo and Scilla Elworthy, Minority Rights Group International, London, 1992. ISBN 0-946690-90-1

[17] "Maternal and child health and family planning: traditional practices harmful to the health of women and children", adopted at the 47th World Health Assembly

[18] *Female Genital Mutilation: Proposals for change*

[19] World Medical Association Statement on Condemnation of Female Genital Mutilation, adopted by the 45th World Medical Assembly, Budapest, Hungary, October 1993

[20] *Female Genital Mutilation: Proposals for Change*

[21] *Ibid*

UN CONVENTION ON THE ELIMINATION OF ALL FORMS OF DISCRIMINATION AGAINST WOMEN (1979)

The State Parties to the present Convention,

Noting that the Charter of the United Nations reaffirms faith in fundamental human rights, in the dignity and worth of the human person and in the equal rights of men and women,

Noting that the Universal Declaration of Human Rights affirms the principle of the inadmissibility of discrimination and proclaims that all human beings are born free and equal in dignity and rights and that everyone is entitled to all the rights and freedoms set forth therein, without distinction of any kind, including distinction based on sex,

Noting that the States Parties to the International Covenants on Human Rights have the obligation to ensure the equal right of men and women to enjoy all economic, social, cultural, civil and political rights,

Considering the international conventions concluded under the auspices of the United Nations and the specialized agencies promoting equality of rights of men and women,

Noting also the resolutions, declarations and recommendations adopted by the United Nations and the specialized agencies promoting equality of rights of men and women,

Concerned, however, that despite these various instruments extensive discrimination against women continues to exist,

Recalling that discrimination against women violates the principles of equality of rights and respect for human dignity, is an obstacle to the participation of women, on equal terms with men, in the political, social, economic and cultural life of their countries, hampers the growth of the prosperity of society and the family and makes more difficult the full development of the potentialities of women in the service of their countries and of humanity,

Concerned that in situations of poverty women have the least access to food, health, education, training, and opportunities for employment and other needs,

Convinced that the establishment of the new international economic order based on equity and justice will contribute significantly towards the promotion of equality between men and women,

Emphasizing that the eradication of apartheid, of all forms of racism, racial discrimination, colonialism, neo-colonialism, aggression, foreign occupation and domination and interference in the internal affairs of States is essential to the full enjoyment of the rights of men and women,

Affirming that the strengthening of international peace and security, relaxation of international tension, mutual co-operation among all States irrespective of their social and economic systems, general and complete disarmament, and in particular nuclear disarmament under strict and effective international control, the affirmation of the principles of justice, equality and mutual benefit in relations among countries and the realization of the right of peoples under alien and colonial domination and foreign occupation to self-determination and independence, as well as respect for national sovereignty and territorial integrity, will promote social progress and development and as a consequence will contribute to the attainment of full equality between men and women,

Convinced that the full and complete development of a country, the welfare of the world and the cause of peace require the maximum participation of women on equal terms with men in all fields,

Bearing in mind the great contribution of women to the welfare of the family and to the development of society, so far not fully recognized, the social significance of maternity and the role of both parents in the family and in the upbringing of children, and aware that the role of women in procreation should not be a basis for discrimination but that the upbringing of children requires a sharing of responsibility between men and women and society as a whole,

Aware that a change in the traditional role of men as well as the role of women in society and in the family is needed to achieve full equality between men and women,

Determined to implement the principles set forth in the Declaration on the Elimination of Discrimination against Women and, for that purpose, to adopt the measures required for the elimination of such discrimination in all its forms and manifestations,

Have agreed on the following:

PART I

Article 1

For the purposes of the present Convention, the term "discrimination against women" shall mean any distinction, exclusion or restriction made on the basis of sex which has the effect or purpose of impairing or nullifying the recognition, enjoyment or exercise by women, irrespective of their marital status, on a basis of equality of men and women, of human rights and fundamental freedoms in the political, economic, social, cultural, civil or any other field.

Article 2

States Parties condemn discrimination against women in all its forms, agree to pursue by all appropriate means and without delay a policy of eliminating discrimination against women and, to this end, undertake:

(a) To embody the principle of the equality of men and women in their national constitutions or other appropriate legislation if not yet incorporated therein and to ensure, through law and other appropriate means, the practical realization of this principle;

(b) To adopt appropriate legislative and other measures, including sanctions where appropriate, prohibiting all discrimination against women;

(c) To establish legal protection of the rights of women on an equal basis with men and to ensure through competent national tribunals and other public institutions the effective protection of women against any act of discrimination;

(d) To refrain from engaging in any act or practice of discrimination against women and to ensure that public authorities and institutions shall act in conformity with this obligation;

(e) To take all appropriate measures to eliminate discrimination against women by any person, organization or enterprise;

(f) To take all appropriate measures, including legislation, to modify or abolish existing laws, regulations, customs and practices which constitute discrimination against women;

(g) To repeal all national penal provisions which constitute discrimination against women.

Article 3

States Parties shall take in all fields, in particular in the political, social, economic and cultural fields, all appropriate measures, including legislation, to ensure the full development and advancement of women, for the purpose of guaranteeing them the exercise and enjoyment of human rights and fundamental freedoms on a basis of equality with men.

Article 4

1. Adoption by States Parties of temporary special measures aimed at accelerating *de facto* equality between men and women shall not be considered discrimination as defined in the present Convention, but shall in no way entail as a consequence the maintenance of unequal or separate standards; these measures shall be discontinued when the objectives of equality of opportunity and treatment have been achieved.

2. Adoption by States Parties of special measures, including those measures contained in the present Convention, aimed at protecting maternity shall not be considered discriminatory.

Article 5

States Parties shall take all appropriate measures:

1. To modify the social and cultural patterns of conduct of men and women, with a view to achieving the elimination of prejudices and customary and all other practices which are based on the idea of the inferiority or superiority of either of the sexes or on stereotyped roles for men and women;

2. To ensure that family education includes a proper understanding of maternity as a social function and the recognition of the common responsibility of men and women in the upbringing and development of their children, it being understood that the interest of the children is the primordial consideration in all cases.

Article 6

States Parties shall take all appropriate measures, including legislation, to suppress all forms of traffic in women and exploitation of prostitution of women.

PART II

Article 7

States Parties shall take all appropriate measures to eliminate discrimination against women in the political and public life of the country and, in particular, shall ensure to women, on equal terms with men, the right:

(a) To vote in all elections and public referenda and to be eligible for election to all publicly elected bodies;

(b) To participate in the formulation of government policy and the implementation thereof and to hold public office and perform all public functions at all levels of government;

To participate in non-governmental organizations and associations concerned with the public and political life of the country.

Article 8

States Parties shall take all appropriate measures to ensure to women, on equal terms with men and without any discrimination, the opportunity to represent their Governments at the international level and to participate in the work of international organizations.

Article 9

1. States Parties shall grant women equal rights with men to acquire, change or retain their nationality. They shall ensure in particular that neither marriage to an alien nor change of nationality by the husband during marriage shall automatically change the nationality of the wife, render her stateless or force upon her the nationality of the husband.

2. States Parties shall grant women equal rights with men with respect to the nationality of their children.

PART III

Article 10

States Parties shall take all appropriate measures to eliminate discrimination against women in order to ensure them equal rights with men in the field of education and in particular to ensure, on a basis of equality of men and women:

(a) The same conditions for career and vocational guidance, for access to studies and for the achievement of diplomas in educational establishments of all categories in rural as well as in urban areas; this equality shall be ensured in pre-school, general, technical, professional and higher technical education, as well as in all types of vocational training;

(b) Access to the same curricula, the same examinations, teaching staff with qualifications of the same standard and school premises and equipment of the same quality;

(c) The elimination of any stereotyped concept of the roles of men and women at all levels and in all forms of education by encouraging coeducation and other types of education which will help to achieve this aim and, in particular, by the revision of textbooks and school programmes and the adaptation of teaching methods;

(d) The same opportunities to benefit from scholarship and other study grants;

(e) The same opportunities for access to programmes of continuing education, including adult and functional literacy programmes, particularly those aimed at reducing, at the earliest possible time, any gap in education existing between men and women;

(f) The reduction of female student drop-out rates and the organization of programmes for girls and women who have left school prematurely;

(g) The same opportunities to participate actively in sports and physical education;

(h) Access to specific educational information to help ensure the health and well-being of families, including information and advice on family planning.

Article 11

1. States Parties shall take all appropriate measures to eliminate discrimination against women in the field of employment in order to ensure, on a basis of equality of men and women, the same rights, in particular:

(a) The right to work as an inalienable right of all human beings;

(b) The right to the same employment opportunities, including the application of the same criteria for selection in matters of employment;

(c) The right to free choice of profession and employment, the right to promotion, job security and all benefits and conditions of service and the right to receive vocational training and retraining, including apprenticeships, advanced vocational training and recurrent training;

(d) The right to equal remuneration, including benefits, and to equal treatment in respect of work of equal value, as well as equality of treatment in the evaluation of the quality of work;

(e) The right to social security, particularly in cases of retirement, unemployment, sickness, invalidity and old age and other incapacity to work, as well as the right to paid leave;

(f) The right to protection of health and to safety in working conditions, including the safeguarding of the function of reproduction.

2. In order to prevent discrimination against women on the grounds of marriage or maternity and to ensure their effective right to work, States Parties shall take appropriate measures:

(a) To prohibit, subject to the imposition of sanctions, dismissal on the grounds of pregnancy or of maternity leave and discrimination in dismissals on the basis of marital status;

(b) To introduce maternity leave with pay or with comparable social benefits without loss of former employment, seniority or social allowances;

(c) To encourage the provision of the necessary supporting social services to enable parents to combine family obligations with work responsibilities and participation in public life, in particular through promoting the establishment and development of a network of child-care facilities;

(d) To provide special protection to women during pregnancy in types of work proved to be harmful to them.

2. Protect legislation relating to matters covered in this article shall be reviewed periodically in the light of scientific and technological knowledge and shall be revised, repealed or extended as necessary.

Article 12

1. States Parties shall take all appropriate measures to eliminate discrimination against women in the field of health care in order to ensure, on a basis of equality of men and women, access to health care services, including those related to family planning.

2. Notwithstanding the provisions of paragraph 1 of this article, States Parties shall ensure to women appropriate services in connection with pregnancy, confinement and the post-natal period, granting free services where necessary, as well as adequate nutrition during pregnancy and lactation.

Article 13

States Parties shall take all appropriate measures to eliminate discrimination against women in other areas of economic and social life in order to ensure, on a basis of equality of men and women, the same rights, in particular:

(a) The right to family benefits;

(b) The right to bank loans, mortgages and other forms of financial credit;

(c) The right to participate in recreational activities, sports and all aspects of cultural life.

Article 14

1. States Parties shall take into account the particular problems faced by rural women and the significant roles which rural women play in the economic survival of their families, including their work in the non-monetized sectors of the economy, and shall take all appropriate measures to ensure the application of the provisions of this Convention to women in rural areas.

2. States Parties shall take all appropriate measures to eliminate discrimination against women in rural areas in order to ensure, on a basis of equality of men and women, that they participate in and benefit from rural development and, in particular, shall ensure to such women the right:

(a) To participate in the elaboration and implementation of development planning at all levels;

(b) To have access to adequate health care facilities, including information, counselling and services in family planning;

(c) To benefit directly from social security programmes;

(d) To obtain all types of training and education, formal and non-formal, including that relating to functional literacy, as well as, *inter alia*, the benefit of all community and extension services, in order to increase their technical proficiency;

(e) To organize self-help groups and co-operatives in order to obtain equal access to economic opportunities through employment or self-employment;

(f) To participate in all community activities;

(g) To have access to agricultural credit and loans, marketing facilities, appropriate technology and equal treatment in land and agrarian reform as well as in land resettlement schemes;

(h) To enjoy adequate living conditions, particularly in relation to housing, sanitation, electricity and water supply, transport and communications.

PART IV

Article 15

1. States Parties shall accord to women equality with men before the law.

2. States Parties shall accord to women, in civil matters, a legal capacity identical to that of men and the same opportunities to exercise that capacity. In particular, they shall give women equal rights to conclude contracts and administer property and shall treat them equally in all stages of procedure in courts and tribunals.

3. States Parties agree that all contracts and all other private instruments of any kind with a legal effect which is directed at restricting the legal capacity of women shall be deemed null and void.

4. States Parties shall accord to men and women the same rights with regard to the law relating to the movement of persons and the freedom to choose their residence and domicile.

Article 16

1. States Parties shall take all appropriate measures to eliminate discrimination against women in all matters relating to marriage and family relations and in particular shall ensure, on a basis of equality of men and women:

(a) The same right to enter into marriage;

(b) The same right freely to choose a spouse and to enter into marriage only with their free and full consent;

(c) The same rights and responsibilities during marriage and at its dissolution;

(d) The same rights and responsibilities as parents, irrespective of their marital status, in matters relating to their children; in all cases the interests of the children shall be paramount;

(e) The same rights to decide freely and responsibly on the number and spacing of their children and to have access to the information, education and means to enable them to exercise these rights;

(f) The same rights and responsibilities with regard to guardianship, wardship, trusteeship and adoption of children, or similar institutions where these concepts exist in national legislation; in all cases the interests of the children shall be paramount;

(g) The same personal rights as husband and wife, including the right to choose a family name, a profession and an occupation;

(h) The same rights for both spouses in respect of the ownership, acquisition, management, administration, enjoyment and disposition of property, whether free of charge or for a valuable consideration.

2. The betrothal and the marriage of a child shall have no legal effect, and all necessary action, including legislation, shall be taken to specify a minimum age for marriage and to make the registration of marriages in an official registry compulsory.

The remaining articles are summarized below:

Article 17 calls for the establishment of the Committee on the Elimination of Discrimination against Women (CEDAW) which will evaluate progress made in implementation of the Convention.

Article 18 establishes a schedule of reporting on progress by ratifying countries.

Article 19 establishes a term of two years for officers of CEDAW.

Article 20 establishes a cycle of meetings to review reports of ratifying countries.

Article 21 directs CEDAW to make general recommendations based on reports.

Article 22 allows for specialized agencies to submit reports that fall within the scope of their activities.

Articles 23–30 detail administration of the Convention.

UN DECLARATION ON THE ELIMINATION OF VIOLENCE AGAINST WOMEN (DECEMBER 1993)

The General Assembly,

Recognizing the urgent need for the universal application to women of the rights and principles with regard to equality, security, liberty, integrity and dignity of all human beings,

Noting that those rights and principles are enshrined in international instruments, including the Universal Declaration of Human Rights,[1] the International Covenant on Civil and Political Rights,[2] the International Covenant on Economic, Social and Cultural Rights,[2] the Convention on the Elimination of All Forms of Discrimination against Women[3] and the Convention against Torture and Other Cruel, Inhuman or Degrading Treatment or Punishment,[4]

Recognizing that effective implementation of the Convention on the Elimination of All Forms of Discrimination against Women would contribute to the elimination of violence against women and that the Declaration on the Elimination of Violence against Women, set forth in the present resolution, will strengthen and complement that process,

Concerned that violence against women is an obstacle to the achievement of equality, development and peace, as recognized in the Nairobi Forward-looking Strategies for the Advancement of Women,[5] in which a set of measures to combat violence against women was recommended, and to the full implementation of the Convention on the Elimination of All Forms of Discrimination against Women,

Affirming that violence against women constitutes a violation of the rights and fundamental freedoms of women and impairs or nullifies their enjoyment of those rights and freedoms, and concerned about the long-standing failure to protect and promote those rights and freedoms in the case of violence against women,

Recognizing that violence against women is a manifestation of historically unequal power relations between men and women, which have led to domination over and discrimination against women by men and to the prevention of the full advancement of women, and that violence against women is one of the crucial social mechanisms by which women are forced into a subordinate position compared with men,

Concerned that some groups of women, such as women belonging to minority groups, indigenous women, refugee women, migrant women, women living in rural or remote communities, destitute women, women in institutions or in detention, female children, women with disabilities, elderly women and women in situations of armed conflict, are especially vulnerable to violence,

Recalling the conclusion in paragraph 23 of the annex to Economic and Social Council resolution 1990/15 of 24 May 1990 that the recognition that violence against women in the family and society was pervasive and cut across lines of income, class and culture had to be matched by urgent and effective steps to eliminate its incidence,

Recalling also Economic and Social Council resolution 1991/18 of 30 May 1991, in which the Council recommended the development of a framework for an international instrument that would address explicitly the issue of violence against women,

Welcoming the role that women's movements are playing in drawing increasing attention to the nature, severity and magnitude of the problem of violence against women,

Alarmed that opportunities for women to achieve legal, social, political and economic equality in society are limited, *inter alia*, by continuing and endemic violence,

Convinced that in the light of the above there is a need for a clear and comprehensive definition of violence against women, a clear statement of the rights to be applied to ensure the elimination of violence against women in all its forms, a commitment by States in respect of their responsibilities, and a commitment by the international community at large to the elimination of violence against women,

Solemnly proclaims the following Declaration on the Elimination of Violence against Women and urges that every effort be made so that it becomes generally known and respected:

Article 1

For the purpose of this Declaration, the term "violence against women" means any act of gender-based violence that results in, or is likely to result in, physical, sexual or psychological harm or suffering to women, including threats of such acts, coercion or arbitrary deprivation of liberty, whether occurring in public or in private life.

Article 2

Violence against women shall be understood to encompass, but not be limited to, the following:

(a) Physical, sexual and psychological violence occurring in the family, including battering, sexual abuse of female children in the household, dowry-related violence, marital rape, female genital mutilation and other traditional practices harmful to women, non-spousal violence and violence related to exploitation;

(b) Physical, sexual and psychological violence occurring within the general community, including rape, sexual abuse, sexual harassment and intimidation at work, in educational institutions and elsewhere, trafficking in women and forced prostitution;

(c) Physical, sexual and psychological violence perpetrated or condoned by the State, wherever it occurs.

Article 3

Women are entitled to the equal enjoyment and protection of all human rights and fundamental freedoms in the political, economic, ocial, cultural, civil or any other field. These rights include, *inter alia*:

(a) The right to life;[6]

(b) The right to equality;[7]

(c) The right to liberty and security of person;[8]

(d) The right to equal protection under the law;[7]

(e) The right to be free from all forms of discrimination;[7]

(f) The right to the highest standard attainable of physical and mental health;[9]

(g) The right to just and favourable conditions of work;[10]

(h) The right not to be subjected to torture, or other cruel, inhuman or degrading treatment or punishment.[11]

Article 4

States should condemn violence against women and should not invoke any custom, tradition or religious consideration to avoid their obligations with respect to its elimination. States should pursue by all appropriate means and without delay a policy of eliminating violence against women and, to this end, should:

(a) Consider, where they have not yet done so, ratifying or acceding to the Convention on the Elimination of All Forms of Discrimination against Women or withdrawing reservations to that Convention;

(b) Refrain from engaging in violence against women;

(c) Exercise due diligence to prevent, investigate and, in accordance with national legislation, punish acts of violence against women, whether those acts are perpetrated by the State or by private persons;

(d) Develop penal, civil, labour and administrative sanctions in domestic legislation to punish and redress the wrongs caused to women who are subjected to violence; women who are subjected to violence should be provided with access to the mechanisms of justice and, as provided for by national legislation, to just and effective remedies for the harm that they have suffered; States should also inform women of their rights in seeking redress through such mechanisms;

(e) Consider the possibility of developing national plans of action to promote the protection of women against any form of violence, or to include provisions for that purpose in plans already existing, taking into account, as appropriate, such cooperation as can be provided by non-governmental organizations, particularly those concerned with the issue of violence against women;

(f) Develop, in a comprehensive way, preventive approaches and all those measures of a legal, political, administrative and cultural nature that promote the protection of women against any form of violence, and ensure that the re-victimization of women does not occur because of laws insensitive to gender considerations, enforcement practices or other interventions;

(g) Work to ensure, to the maximum extent feasible in the light of their available resources and, where needed, within the framework of international cooperation, that women subjected to violence and, where appropriate, their children have specialized assistance, such as rehabilitation, assistance in child care and maintenance, treatment, counselling, and health and social services, facilities and programmes, as well as support structures, and should take all other appropriate measures to promote their safety and physical and psychological rehabilitation;

(h) Include in government budgets adequate resources for their activities related to the elimination of violence against women;

(i) Take measures to ensure that law enforcement officers and public officials responsible for implementing policies to prevent, investigate and punish violence against women receive training to sensitize them to the needs of women;

(j) Adopt all appropriate measures, especially in the field of education, to modify the social and cultural patterns of conduct of men and women and to eliminate prejudices, customary practices and all other practices based on the idea of the inferiority or superiority of either of the sexes and on stereotyped roles for men and women;

(k) Promote research, collect data and compile statistics, especially concerning domestic violence, relating to the prevalence of different forms of violence against women and encourage research on the causes, nature, seriousness and consequences of violence against women and on the effectiveness of measures implemented to prevent and redress violence against women; those statistics and findings of the research will be made public;

(l) Adopt measures directed towards the elimination of violence against women who are especially vulnerable to violence;

(m) Include, in submitting reports as required under relevant human rights instruments of the United Nations, information pertaining to violence against women and measures taken to implement the present Declaration;

(n) Encourage the development of appropriate guidelines to assist in the implementation of the principles set forth in the present Declaration;

(o) Recognize the important role of the women's movement and non-governmental organizations world wide in raising awareness and alleviating the problem of violence against women;

(p) Facilitate and enhance the work of the women's movement and non-governmental organizations and cooperate with them at local, national and regional levels;

(q) Encourage intergovernmental regional organizations of which they are members to include the elimination of violence against women in their programmes, as appropriate.

Article 5

The organs and specialized agencies of the United Nations system should, with their respective fields of competence, contribute to the recognition and realization of the rights and the principles set forth in the present Declaration and, to this end, should *inter alia*:

(a) Foster international and regional cooperation with a view to defining regional strategies for combating violence, exchanging experiences and financing programmes relating to the elimination of violence against women;

(b) Promote meetings and seminars with the aim of creating and raising awareness among all persons of the issue of the elimination of violence against women;

(c) Foster coordination and exchange within the United Nations system between human rights treaty bodies to address the issue of violence against women effectively;

(d) Include in analyses prepared by organizations and bodies of the United Nations system of social trends and problems, such as the periodic reports on the world social situation, examination of trends in violence against women;

(e) Encourage coordination between organizations and bodies of the United Nations system to incorporate the issue of violence against women into ongoing programmes, especially with reference to groups of women particularly vulnerable to violence;

(f) Promote the formulation of guidelines or manuals relating to violence against women, taking into account the measures referred to in the present Declaration;

(g) Consider the issue of the elimination of violence against women, as appropriate, in fulfilling their mandates with respect to the implementation of human rights instruments;

(h) Cooperate with non-governmental organizations in addressing the issue of violence against women.

Article 6

Nothing in the present Declaration shall affect any provision that is more conducive to the elimination of violence against women that may be contained in the legislation of a State or in any international convention, treaty or other instrument in force in a State.

85th plenary meeting
20 December 1993

1 Resolution 217 A (III).
2 See resolution 2200 A (XXI), annex.
3 Resolution 34/180, annex.
4 Resolution 39/46, annex.
5 *Report of the World Conference to Review and Appraise the Achievements of the United Nations Decade for Women: Equality, Development and Peace, Nairobi, 15-26 July 1985* (United Nations publication, Sales No. E.85.IV.10), chap. I, sect. A.
6 Universal Declaration of Human Rights, article 3; and International Covenant on Civil and Political Rights, article 6.
7 International Covenant on Civil and Political Rights, article 26.
8 Universal Declaration of Human Rights, article 3; and International Covenant on Civil and Political Rights, article 9.
9 International Covenant on Economic, Social and Cultural Rights, article 12.
10 Universal Declaration of Human Rights, article 23; and International Covenant on Economic, Social and Cultural Rights, articles 6 and 7.
11 Universal Declaration of Human Rights, article 5; International Covenant on Civil and Political Rights, article 7; and Convention against Torture and Other Cruel, Inhuman or Degrading Treatment or Punishment.